PRAISE FOR
The Art of Simple Living

"Shunmyo Masuno's simple and relevant practices land gently and with the most comforting ordinariness, like a warm breath of familiarity to us, the frazzled masses."

> —Sarah Wilson, *New York Times* bestselling author of *First, We Make the Beast Beautiful*

"Our mind is blazing in the new dopamine war between alarmist news and attention-hooking apps. *The Art of Simple Living* is a bucket of water on the flames."

> —Neil Pasricha, *New York Times* bestselling author of *The Book of Awesome* and *The Happiness Equation*

"I love this book. These little Zen practices can bring so much serenity to your life."

> —Francine Jay, bestselling author of *The Joy of Less* and *Lightly*

"An encouraging and straightforward companion for all who seek to amplify the inherent peace of their minds."

> —Dzogchen Ponlop Rinpoche, author of *Emotional Rescue* and *Rebel Buddha*

"This little treasure needs to be at every bedside."

> —Allan Lokos, founder and guiding teacher, Community Meditation Center, NYC; author of *Through the Flames, Patience,* and *Pocket Peace*

PENGUIN BOOKS

THE ART OF SIMPLE LIVING

Shunmyo Masuno is the head priest of a 450-year-old Zen Buddhist temple in Japan, an award-winning Zen garden designer for clients all over the world, and a professor of environmental design at one of Japan's leading art schools. He has lectured widely, including at the Harvard Graduate School of Design, Cornell University, and Brown University.

The Art of
SIMPLE
LIVING

*100 Daily Practices from
a Japanese Zen Monk
for a Lifetime of
Calm and Joy*

SHUNMYO MASUNO

Translated by ALLISON MARKIN POWELL

Artwork by HARRIET LEE-MERRION

PENGUIN BOOKS

PENGUIN BOOKS
An imprint of Penguin Random House LLC
penguinrandomhouse.com

Originally published in Japanese as *Zen, Simple Seikatsu No Susume*
by Mikasa-Shobo Publishers Co., Ltd., Tokyo.

This English-language edition is published by arrangement with
Mikasa-Shobo Publishers Co., Ltd., Tokyo c/o Tuttle-Mori Agency, Inc., Tokyo.

Illustrations by Harriet Lee-Merrion

ISBN 9780143134046 (hardcover)
ISBN 9780525505846 (ebook)

Printed in the United States of America
1   3   5   7   9   10   8   6   4   2

Set in Berling with Diotima Classic
Text design by Sabrina Bowers

CONTENTS

PART TWO

30 ways to inspire confidence and courage for living

Try changing your perspective.

PART THREE

20 ways to alleviate confusion and worry

Try changing how you interact with others.

PART FOUR

20 ways to make any day the best day

Try shifting your attention to the present moment.

FOREWORD

Just subtle shifts in your habits and perspective.
That's all you need to live simply.

You visit a temple or shrine in an ancient city, and look out at the tranquil gardens.

You break a sweat climbing a mountain, and enjoy the sweeping vista from the summit.

You stand before a crystal blue sea, and just stare out at the horizon.

Have you experienced this sense of being refreshed, in such extraordinary moments when you are removed from the hustle and bustle of everyday life?

Your heart feels lighter, and a warm energy surges through your body. The worries and stresses of daily life vanish for an instant, and you can just feel yourself, alive in this moment.

Nowadays, many people have lost their footing—they are worried and confused about how to live their lives. That is why they seek out the extraordinary, in an attempt to reset their mental balance.

But. Still.

Even once you have pushed reset, the extraordinary remains outside of the everyday.

When you return to your regular life, stress accumulates, and the mind frays. Feeling burdened, again you seek out the extraordinary. Does this never-ending cycle sound familiar?

No matter how much you lament the complexities of life, changing the world is no simple task.

If the world is not going the way you want it to, perhaps it is better to change yourself.

Then, whatever world you encounter, you can move through it comfortably and with ease.

Instead of going out of your way to seek the extraordinary, what if you could live in a more carefree way, just by subtly changing your regular, everyday life?

This book is about just that: simple living, Zen style.

Changing your lifestyle doesn't need to be difficult.

Slight changes in your habits. A subtle shift in your perspective.

You don't need to go to the ancient Japanese capitals of Kyoto or Nara; you don't need to climb Mount Fuji; and you don't need to live near the ocean. With really only minor effort, it is possible to savor the extraordinary.

In this book, I will show you how to do so, with the help of Zen.

Zen is based on teachings that are fundamentally about how humans can live in the world.

In other words, Zen is about habits, ideas, and hints for living a happy life. A treasure trove, if you will, of deep yet simple life wisdom.

Zen teaching is represented by a series of four phrases, which mean, essentially: "Spiritual awakening is transmitted outside of the sutras, and cannot be experienced through words or letters; Zen points directly to the human mind, and enables you to perceive your true nature and attain Buddhahood." Rather than be fixated on the written or spoken word, we should encounter our essential selves as they exist in the here and now.

Try not to be swayed by the values of others, not to be troubled by unnecessary concerns, but to live an infinitely simple life, stripped of wasteful things. That is "Zen style."

Once you adopt these habits—which I promise are simple—your worries will disappear.

Once you develop this simple practice, life becomes so much more relaxed.

It is precisely because of how complex the world is that Zen offers these hints for living.

Nowadays, Zen is receiving more and more attention, not only in Japan but abroad as well.

I serve as the head priest of a Zen temple, and I also work as a Zen garden designer—not just for Zen temples but also for hotels and foreign embassies and such. Zen gardens are not just for Japanese people—they transcend religion and nationality and can capture the hearts of Westerners as well.

Rather than frown at the idea of Zen, try simply standing before one of these gardens. It can refresh your mind and spirit. The chatter and ripples in your mind suddenly grow silent and still.

I find that encountering a Zen garden can convey far more about Zen concepts than reading any number of texts explaining the philosophy.

That is why I have chosen to make this book practical. Instead of merely understanding Zen intellectually, I hope you will adopt the book's practices as your own sort of training.

Keep this book by your side, and whenever anxiety or worries rear their head, turn to these pages.

The answers you seek are within.

Gassho
SHUNMYO MASUNO

PART ONE

30 WAYS TO ENERGIZE YOUR "PRESENT SELF"

Try making a subtle shift in your habits.

1

MAKE TIME FOR EMPTINESS.

First, observe yourself.

Be with yourself as you are,
but without haste, without impatience.

In our everyday lives, do any of us have time to think about nothing?

I imagine most people would say, "I don't have a moment to spare for that."

We're pressed for time, pressured by work and everything else in our lives. Modern life is busier than ever. All day, every day, we try our best just to do what has to get done.

If we immerse ourselves in this kind of routine, unconsciously but inevitably we lose sight of our true selves, and of true happiness.

Any given day, a mere ten minutes is all you need. Try making time for emptiness, for not thinking about anything.

Just try clearing your mind, and not being caught up in the things around you.

Various thoughts will float up in your mind, but try to send them away, one by one. When you do so, you will begin to notice the present moment, the subtle shifts in nature that are keeping you alive. When you are not distracted by other things, your pure and honest self can be revealed.

Making time for not thinking about anything. That is the first step toward creating a simple life.

2

WAKE UP FIFTEEN MINUTES EARLIER.

*The prescription for when
there is no room in your heart*

How being busy makes you lose heart

When we are short on time, this scarcity extends to our heart as well. We automatically say, "I'm busy—I don't have time." When we feel this way, our mind becomes even more hectic.

But are we really so busy? Aren't we the ones who are pushing ourselves to hurry?

In Japanese, the character for "busy" is written with the symbols for "lose" and "heart."

It's not that we are busy because there isn't enough time. We are busy because there is no room in our heart.

Especially when things are hectic, try waking up fifteen minutes earlier than usual. Lengthen your spine, and take slow breaths from the point below your navel—the spot we refer to as the *tanden*. Once your breathing is in order, your mind will naturally settle into stillness as well.

Then, while you enjoy a cup of tea or coffee, look out the window at the sky. Try to listen for the warbling of little birds.

How peculiar—just like that, you create space in your mind.

Waking up fifteen minutes earlier magically liberates you from busyness.

3

SAVOR THE MORNING AIR.

The monk's secret to a long life is found here.

Each day is not the same.

It is said that Buddhist monks who practice Zen live long lives.

Of course, diet and breathing techniques are contributing factors, but I believe that a regular and orderly lifestyle exerts a positive influence, both spiritually and physically.

I rise each morning at 5:00, and the first thing I do is fill my lungs with the morning air. As I walk around the temple's main hall, reception hall, and priest's quarters, opening the rain shutters, my body experiences the changes of the seasons. At 6:30 I perform the Buddhist liturgy by chanting scripture, and then I have breakfast. What follows is whatever the business of that particular day is.

The same process repeats itself every day, but each day is not the same. The taste of the morning air, the moment when the morning sunlight arrives, the touch of the breeze on your cheek, the color of the sky and of the leaves on the trees—everything is constantly shifting. Morning is the time when you can thoroughly experience these changes.

This is why monks perform zazen meditation before dawn, in order to physically experience these changes in nature.

With the first zazen practice of the day, *kyoten* zazen—morning zazen—we nourish our mind and body by breathing in the beautiful morning air.

4

LINE UP YOUR SHOES
WHEN YOU TAKE THEM OFF.

This will beautify your life.

Disorder in your mind shows in your feet.

It has long been said that you can tell a lot about a household by looking at its entrance hall, especially in Japanese homes, where we remove our shoes upon entering. If the footwear is perfectly lined up, or if it is all ajumble—you can know the state of mind of those who live there by just this one detail.

In Zen Buddhism we have a saying that means "Look carefully at what is under your own feet." It has a literal meaning, but it also suggests that those who do not pay attention to their footsteps cannot know themselves, and cannot know where their life is going. This may sound like an exaggeration, but such a small thing really can have a tremendous influence on the way you live.

When you come home, take off your shoes and line them up neatly by the front door. Just this one thing. It takes only three seconds.

Yet by cultivating this habit, everything about your life will be inexplicably sharper and more orderly. It will beautify your life. This is human nature.

First, try turning your attention to your feet.

By lining up your shoes, you are taking the next step toward where you are going.

5

DISCARD WHAT YOU DON'T NEED.

It will refresh your mind.

*Part with old things
before acquiring new ones.*

When things aren't going well, we tend to think we are lacking in something. But if we want to change our current situation, we should first part with something before we look to acquire something else. This is a fundamental tenet of simple living.

Discard your attachments. Let go of your assumptions. Reduce your possessions. Living simply is also about discarding your physical and mental burdens.

It's amazing how refreshed we can feel after a good cry. Crying clears out whatever weight you were carrying in your heart. You feel energized to try again. I have always felt that the Buddhist concept of the "enlightened mind"—the Japanese characters for which depict a "clean mind"—refers to this "refreshment" of the spirit.

The act of discarding, of detaching from mental and physical burdens, from the baggage that weighs us down, is extremely difficult. Sometimes it can be accompanied by real pain, as when we part with someone who is dear to us.

But if you want to improve the way things are, if you want to live with a light heart, you must start by discarding. The moment you detach, a new abundance will flow into your life.

6

ORGANIZE YOUR DESKTOP.

Cleaning hones the mind.

Your desk is a mirror that reflects your inner mind.

Take a look at the desks around you at the office. The people who always have tidy desktops are most likely good at their jobs. In contrast, those whose desks are always cluttered may be unsettled and have trouble focusing on their work.

When things get out of order, straighten them out. When things get messy, clean them up. Before you finish work for the day, tidy up and straighten out your desktop. People who are in the habit of doing so feel more clearheaded. They are able to focus one hundred percent, without distraction, on their work.

In Zen temples, monks do cleaning every morning and every evening. We clean with all our heart, though not because the temple is dirty. The purpose is not only to make the temple sparkle, but also to polish our minds through the act of cleaning.

With every sweep of the broom, you clear out the dust in your mind.

With every swipe of the cloth, your heart gleams brighter.

This applies to your desk at the office as well as to the rooms in your home. Do not allow yourself to be disrupted by your anxieties or troubles—the key to keeping your mind invigorated is to first put the things around you in order.

7

MAKE A DELICIOUS CUP OF COFFEE.

The happiness to be found in taking your time

When we eliminate effort,
we eliminate life's pleasures.

What do you do when you want a cup of coffee? If you're at home, you turn on the coffeemaker. Or if you're out, you get a cheap cup of coffee. These are both perfectly natural.

But imagine a different scenario.

First, you go out into the woods and collect firewood. You make a fire and boil water. As you grind the coffee beans, you look up at the sky and say, "What a beautiful day."

Coffee brewed this way is likely to taste much better than coffee from a machine. The reason why, perhaps, is because each step in the process has been brought to life—collecting firewood, starting the fire, grinding the beans. There is nothing extraneous in any of these actions. That is what I call living.

Life requires time and effort. That is to say, when we eliminate time and effort, we eliminate life's pleasures.

Every so often, experience the flip side of convenience.

8

PUT PEN TO PAPER WITH CARE.

*Your true self can be seen
in your handwriting.*

Turn your attention inward.

Zen monks have always had an interest in calligraphy and painting.

What do calligraphy and painting represent for us, in particular as part of a Zen practice? Our interest is not in leaving behind work of lasting value, or in taking pride in our skills, but rather in attempting to express ourselves through the artwork.

For example, there is an indescribable intensity in the calligraphy of the celebrated Zen monk Ikkyu. The spirit that is expressed in his work overwhelms those who see it. Similarly, in the landscape paintings of Sesshu, the waves of blurred ink contain the essence of his spirit.

You could say that their calligraphy and paintings are distillations of their inner selves.

The practice of calligraphy and painting is a way of connecting with your inner self. You let go of distractions and simply allow the brush to move across the paper.

Consider trying to write or draw with care—not with the intention of showing it to others, but rather by mindfully facing your inner self.

Your true self will show through, in a single line or letter.

9

TRY USING A LOUD VOICE.

This is a way to
get yourself motivated.

*Speak from your belly and
awaken your brain.*

Have you ever encountered a Zen monk chanting sutras?

His voice resonates in the temple hall as he chants the sutra as an offering at full volume. And if there are several monks chanting, the intensity of their voices seems to reverberate from the very earth.

Why do they chant sutras with such vigor?

There is a good reason.

When you speak loudly, as a matter of course, you are able to hear your own voice clearly. But moreover, it stimulates and activates your brain. We monks rise early and chant sutras first as a means of awakening our brain.

In order to chant loudly, we must assume the proper posture and breathe from the abdomen. Opera singers use the same technique. This is very good for your body. So it makes sense that monks chant sutras so loudly.

Once a day, try using a loud voice, even if you just put a lot of heart into your morning greeting. You may be surprised by how good it feels.

10

DO NOT NEGLECT YOUR MEALS.

Make your meals about the eating.

"Eat and drink with your whole heart."

When you eat, are you focused on the act of eating?

Breakfast is something you race through as you head out the door. Lunch is taken with officemates as you talk about work. And dinner is eaten while watching television. The act of eating is all too often neglected, isn't it?

In Zen Buddhism we have a saying: "Eat and drink with your whole heart." It means that when you drink a cup of tea, focus only on drinking the tea. When you eat a meal, focus only on eating that meal. As you enjoy a dish, think about the people who cooked it. Visualize the field where the vegetables were grown. Feel a sense of gratitude for the bounty of nature.

All our food passes through the hands of a hundred people before it reaches us. By adopting this mind-set as you take your meals, perhaps you will become aware of how fortunate you are.

Why do we take pleasure in delicious things?

Because the life in us savors that which has been cultivated by the life in another.

WHEN EATING,
PAUSE AFTER EVERY BITE.

Savor the sense of gratitude.

Zen practice is not just seated meditation.

The meals of practicing Zen monks are based on Shojin cuisine, or Buddhist vegetarian cuisine. Breakfast, called *shoshoku*, consists of rice porridge and pickles. Lunch, called *tenshin*, is rice and soup, again with pickles. And dinner, called *yakuseki*, is a simple meal, though usually the largest of the day, consisting of a vegetable dish and more rice and soup. Seconds are offered only of rice, and meat is never eaten.

The proper way to take Zen meals involves something called "the Five Reflections." To put it simply:

1. We consider the efforts of those who brought us the food, and are grateful for it.
2. We reflect upon our own actions, and quietly partake.
3. We savor the food, without greed, anger, or obliviousness.
4. We regard the food as medicine to nourish a healthy body and to sustain our spirit.
5. We thankfully receive the food as part of our harmonious path toward enlightenment.

We reflect upon these five things at each meal, expressing gratitude for the food, and we pause after every bite, setting down our chopsticks. The purpose of this pause is to enable us to savor the feelings of gratitude with each bite we take.

Meals are not simply to satisfy hunger. They are an important time to practice our training.

12

DISCOVER THE BENEFITS OF A VEGETABLE-CENTRIC DIET.

*A vegetarian fast is a "quick cleanse"
for your mind and body.*

Inspired by a high priest's beautiful posture

Virtuous monks have a beautiful appearance.

I don't mean that they have an attractive face or that they are stylish; I'm talking about an invigorating beauty that seems to shine through in their skin and body. Their posture, whether seated or standing, is beautiful. Their appearance has been steadily polished by the conscientious daily practice of rising early for Zen training.

There is a direct link between mind and body. When you hone your mind, your renewed vitality naturally shows in your body as well.

Food typically does not serve merely the body. It also has a significant effect on the mind. Food is what creates both your body and your mind.

When you adopt a vegetable-centric diet, your mind becomes peaceful, untroubled by minor irritations. It shows in the clarity of your skin. In contrast, eating nothing but meat inspires a combative spirit. Before you know it, your skin starts to discolor.

I realize that it may be too much to completely eliminate meat and fish from your diet.

My recommendation: Try eating only vegetables one day a week.

13

SEEK OUT YOUR FAVORITE WORDS.

Time for being with your mind

For example, "All things come from nothingness"—a Zen phrase to free yourself from attachments

In the old days, all Japanese homes featured an alcove called a *tokonoma*.

A hanging scroll would be placed in the *tokonoma*, and people could reflect on it whenever they were home. Whether it was a favorite painting or the calligraphy of a guiding principle, the *tokonoma* revealed the spirit and lifestyle of those who lived there.

Consider decorating your home with calligraphy—it could be an inspiring saying, a quote from someone you admire, or something that allows for self-reflection. You don't need an alcove—your living room wall serves just as well. It doesn't matter whether the calligraphy is particularly skillful, either.

Gazing upon it provides time and space for serene contemplation.

If you cannot think of which words to choose, I can suggest these:

"Within nothingness there is infinite potential."

It means that human beings are born possessing nothing. Yet within all of us lies infinite potential.

For this reason, there is nothing to fear. There is nothing to worry about. This is truth.

14

PARE DOWN YOUR BELONGINGS.

Acquire only what you need.

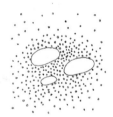

The concept of exhausting
the essence of things

Among the temples in Kyoto, the rock garden at Ryoanji and the grounds at Daisenji serve as exemplary models of Zen gardens.

Both are what are called dry landscape gardens, because they evoke beautiful landscapes without employing ponds or streams or other water elements.

The fact is that even when there is no water present, you can still sense a mountain stream flowing.

In your head, picture a scene with a water element, and allow your mind to linger there.

These gardens are truly representations of our mind set free.

It is not always necessary to have water to convey the idea of it flowing. Eliminate everything extraneous, and create a garden using what you have at hand. Even when you have only one of something, there are various ways you can put it to use with imagination and ingenuity.

In the course of your everyday shopping, before you acquire something new, give some thought to whether you really need it, and take another look at what you already have.

Acquiring lots of things isn't freedom.

What's important is acquiring the mind-set of using things freely.

15

ARRANGE YOUR ROOM SIMPLY.

Doing so will simplify your mind as well

The difference between simplicity and frugality

The relationship between the mind and the body is like that between the chicken and the egg.

If you cultivate a simplified mind-set, your body, too, will naturally become lean. Conversely, if you pay attention to your diet and strengthen your body, your mind, too, will become healthier and stronger.

The same is true about the connection between your mind and your physical space. If you wish to simplify your inner self, arrange your rooms sparely.

A lifestyle of simplicity is what is beautiful. That is the spirit of Zen.

Simplicity is about stripping away what is not useful. Determine whether something is truly necessary, and if it is, then take good care of it. This is different from frugality. Frugality is about subsisting with things of low value. By value, I'm referring not only to its price—it also includes the depth of feeling toward such items.

Living simply means, for instance, that the mug you use every day for coffee is a mug that you really like—one that you take good care of and that you use for a long time. Acquire only good things that will truly be needed. A lifestyle of simplicity is the fundamental practice that will hone the mind.

16

TRY GOING BAREFOOT.

How to keep sickness away

The reason why monks go barefoot

Monks go barefoot 365 days of the year. And the clothes we wear are made of very simple material. Even in the middle of winter, we dress the same way.

For a novice monk, this can be quite a struggle, but once he adjusts, it becomes invigorating. Because this lifestyle naturally strengthens the body, monks rarely catch colds. While a person my age might wear socks during the winter, warm feet are no match for the pleasure of bare feet.

That's why when I go out, I make sure to wear thong sandals.

These are also very good for your health.

It is thought that the area between your big toe and your second toe is where various pressure points related to your internal organs and brain are concentrated. When you wear thong sandals, the straps stimulate these points, and it's like a massage while you are walking.

Go barefoot at home, and wear thong sandals when you go out.

Consider trying this on your days off.

17

EXHALE DEEPLY.

How to eliminate negative emotions

*Improve your breathing, and your mind,
too, will improve.*

In the Japanese word for "breathing," *kokyu*, the character for "breathing out" comes before the character for "breathing in." That is to say, the act of exhaling comes before the act of inhaling.

Focus your awareness on the point below your navel—your *tanden*—as you slowly exhale a long, thin breath. Once you have fully exhaled, inhalation naturally follows. Let your breathing relax, allowing this flow to take over. As the process repeats itself, you will start to feel calmer. Your body will feel more grounded and connected to the earth.

To put it another way, you will be liberated from your restlessness.

When your breathing comes from your chest, you cannot help but feel adrift. It breeds impatience, and your breathing quickens even more. You get caught in a spiral of impatience and irritation.

Whenever you feel a rush of negative emotions, such as anger or anxiety, that is the perfect moment to focus on breathing from your abdomen.

You will soon be more relaxed, and your mind will feel refreshed.

18

SIT ZAZEN.

The effects of sitting and thinking

Humans are not capable of deep reflection
while we are moving

In Zen training, zazen is of the utmost importance. You cannot talk about Zen without zazen. We start with zazen, and we finish with zazen. That is the practice of Zen.

The word *Zen* derives from the Sanskrit word *dhyana*, which means "quiet contemplation."

The act of thinking derives from the concept of sitting quietly. Humans are not capable of thinking while we are moving. We have only one mind, and when our mind is focused on movement, it is difficult for us to engage in profound thought.

Even if you try thinking while you're walking, it will always end up being about something practical, such as work arrangements or what to cook for dinner. Deep contemplation about absolute truth in the world or the meaning of life is not something that can be accomplished while in motion.

For zazen, first we assume the correct posture, next we focus on our breathing, and finally we steady our mind. Once we arrange all three of these things, then we begin to practice zazen.

Try sitting zazen: Empty your mind and allow your thoughts to float up and then drift away.

19

TRY A STANDING PRACTICE.

A Zen-style method to make use of
your commuting time

An easy way to motivate yourself

For people who work outside the home, commuting to the office can be stressful.

But I like to think that a certain amount of time spent commuting can be a good thing.

Imagine if your office and your home were in the same building. You might think it would be convenient, since your commute would take no time at all.

However, we all need to change gears, and living and working in the same building might make this difficult.

In the morning, as you're getting ready to leave for work, you have on your parenting face. Then you walk to the subway, you're jostled on the train, and by the time you arrive at the office, you have on your manager face. Now you're ready to put in another day's hard work.

With your commute as a kind of bridge between your home life and your work life, you're able to assume a completely different mode.

If you'd like a boost to your motivation, I encourage you to try a "standing practice." You can do this even while holding on to the strap in a subway car. As you stand there, focus your awareness on the point below your navel—your *tanden*—and practice zazen. It's simple.

Whether it's during your commute or in a few spare moments during the day, this bit of Zen spiritual practice can be a great help.

20

DON'T WASTE TIME WORRYING ABOUT THINGS YOU CANNOT CONTROL.

*What does it mean to become
spiritually lighter?*

The moment when you suddenly leave yourself behind

When sitting zazen, one mustn't think about anything—that's what we are told, and yet it proves to be quite challenging.

In principle, you do not close your eyes when sitting zazen. Since you can see what is happening around you, you end up having thoughts about something or other, no matter how hard you try. "Oh, the head priest is coming this way. I should sit up straighter . . ." or "Ah, my legs are numb . . ." or various other thoughts that flit through your mind.

Most of the time, this is perfectly natural. And anyway, telling yourself, "Don't think," is itself thinking.

But once you have a bit of experience with zazen, there will be moments—however brief—when your mind is empty. You will realize you aren't thinking about anything. You will even forget about the sense of your "self." These are the very moments I'm talking about.

Your mind will become transparent. The things that usually encumber your thoughts will vanish. You will have the sudden sensation of entering a crystalline world. This is what I mean by becoming spiritually lighter.

21

BECOME ADEPT AT SWITCHING MODES.

Create gates within your mind.

There are such things as
"necessary nonessentials."

The approach to a Zen temple or Shinto shrine always has several gates—large red archways that we call torii.

Before reaching the main hall of a Zen temple, you pass through three gates—the main gate, the central gate, and the triple gate—that represent the journey toward enlightenment. Shinto shrines also have three torii.

Why bother with such superfluous structures?

Well, they are what we call "necessary nonessentials."

We refer to gates and torii as "spiritual barriers." In other words, they connect two separate worlds. As you pass through each one, you come closer to a pure world—what in Buddhism we consider to be "sacred ground."

This is why Buddhist temples feature these three gates. By creating a boundary between worlds, they help you to become aware of the distance between each one. And as you pass through each one, you experience the sensation of crossing over to sacred ground.

You might think of your commute to work as a similar "necessary nonessential." It can provide time for you to switch between your private self and your work self. This may seem superfluous but can be indispensable.

22

BREATHE SLOWLY.

A five-minute "chair zazen"
during your lunch break

*To settle your mind, first adjust your
posture and your breathing.*

When you sit at your desk, your posture inevitably becomes stooped or hunched over. Because this is an inherently unnatural position, it affects your concentration, and you can find the slightest things irritating or fatiguing.

So I have a spiritual practice for you. For five minutes during your lunch break, try doing zazen while sitting in your chair.

The basis for zazen is to harmonize your posture, breathing, and mind.

First, adjust your posture by aligning your head and your tailbone. If you were to see yourself from the side, your spine would create an S-curve, and you could draw a straight line from your head to your tailbone.

Next, attend to your breathing. Under the stressful conditions at work, you might take seven or eight breaths per minute. By focusing on your breathing, you can naturally decrease this to three or four breaths per minute.

Once this happens, your mind will naturally settle.

This practice can make both your head and your heart feel quite refreshed. All it takes is a five-minute "chair zazen" during your lunch break.

23

JOIN YOUR HANDS TOGETHER.

The way to calm an irritable mind

The meaning of gassho: *The left hand represents you; the right represents others.*

There are times when we join our hands together and silently pray for someone or reflect on something. I recommend making time for this not only when you visit a grave or a religious site but in your everyday life as well.

What is *gassho*? The right hand represents anyone other than yourself. It might be the Buddha or God or perhaps someone around you. The left hand represents you. *Gassho* signifies bringing these two together to become one. It is a feeling of respect for those outside of yourself—an offering of humility.

By joining our hands together, we foster a sense of gratitude. It allows no room for conflict. You cannot attack someone when your hands are joined together, can you? An apology given with joined hands soothes anger or irritation. Herein lies the significance of *gassho*.

It's a good idea to designate a space within your home where you can join your hands together. It need not be an altar or a shrine—it can be just a pillar or a corner where you hang an amulet or a talisman—a place you can turn to and silently join your hands together. This small practice can have a surprisingly calming effect on your spirit.

24

MAKE TIME TO BE ALONE.

The first step toward simple living,
Zen style

The benefits of "seclusion in the city"

"Mountain dwelling" is the lifestyle idealized by Japanese people. It is considered the most beautiful and is sometimes referred to as a life sequestered from the world. The famous monks Saigyo and Ryokan were known to have led such hermitic lives.

Reading while listening to the sounds of birds and the rush of water. Enjoying a drink of sake while gazing at the moon's reflection in your glass. Communing with wildlife. The ability to live with a free mind, accepting things for what they are. This is the way of life that has come to be idealized.

As the monk-poet Kamo no Chomei described it in the thirteenth-century work *Hojoki*, mountain dwelling is about living in seclusion, alone in the mountains. Zen Buddhist monks consider this setting to be ideal for spiritual training.

In reality, however, this proves to be quite challenging. Yet still we yearn for the spirit of seclusion.

Adapting the concept of mountain dwelling for modern life, even amid the hustle and bustle of the city, the monk and famous tea master Sen no Rikyu coined the phrase "seclusion in the city." It is this model that explains why teahouses are always set a slight distance away from the main building.

Consider putting into practice the concept of "seclusion in the city."

A place where you can disconnect from other people and spend time by yourself. A place in nature where you can regain mental freedom. A few moments of seclusion can illuminate the path forward.

25

GET IN TOUCH WITH NATURE.

Find the happiness that is right at hand.

Create a miniature garden in your mind.

I once gave a lesson to a group of elementary schoolchildren for a television program.

I suggested that we create miniature gardens.

First I instructed the students to seek out their favorite place in the school and, once there, to try very hard to empty their minds. Then I asked each of them to represent their experiences of nature in a miniature garden.

In a box of about one and a half by two feet, they were free to arrange—however they liked—dirt, pebbles, tree branches, and leaves. I am active as a garden designer, and even from my perspective, the miniature gardens that the children created were truly admirable in their workmanship.

One child conjured up water that flowed into a pond; another child positioned branches on a diagonal, in an attempt to represent wind; and yet another child tried very hard to create shade. . . . These children, whose days were crammed with school and extracurricular activities and enrichment programs, were completely absorbed as they created their miniature gardens. They had a wonderful time engaging with nature.

Try getting in touch with nature yourself. If you notice a stone lying on the ground, pick it up and hold it. When you see flowers blooming by the side of the road, stop and smell their fragrance.

Then, inside your mind, create a miniature garden of your very own. It will relax you.

26

CREATE A SMALL GARDEN ON YOUR BALCONY.

A little place for practicing mindfulness

You can sharpen your mind,
no matter where you are.

We monks say, "Beneath a tree, atop a rock." You sit, alone, on top of a rock or under a tree, and quietly practice zazen. This brings you into communion with nature. You can leave behind whatever thoughts pass through your head and sit zazen with an empty mind. This is the ideal environment for practicing zazen.

It can be challenging even for Buddhist monks to find such a setting. This is why the grounds of Zen temples feature gardens.

We can visualize distant mountains and in our mind can hear the rushing sound of a river. A vast landscape like this can be shrunken to a minuscule version by creating a small garden, and the splendor of nature reproduced within a negligible space. The accumulated wisdom of Buddhist monks is captured in the art of Zen gardens.

Try creating such a garden in your own home. If you don't have a yard, an apartment balcony will do just fine. And if you don't have a balcony, a window ledge will suffice. A few square feet is all you need. Within that space, try representing the landscape of your mind.

A place where your mind can escape. A place where you can look upon your essential self.

It may just become your favorite spot.

27

SEEK OUT THE SUNSET.

Be grateful for making it through
another day.

Find your own "sunset steps."

In a neighborhood of downtown Tokyo called Yanaka, there is a spot that is known as the "sunset steps." These steps are not particularly unusual in and of themselves, but if you take a seat and look up at the sky at the right time, you can catch sight of a beautiful sunset.

I don't know where the name "sunset steps" came from, but at some point everyone just started calling them that. Many people now go there to watch the sunset.

I imagine that there are many such places all over the world. In the Japanese countryside, I bet you can see beautiful sunsets from the footpaths between the rice paddies. And in the city, you can climb up to a rooftop, where the setting sun looms large.

You don't need to go out of your way to get to Yanaka. It's easy to find various places that can serve as your own sunset steps.

The important thing is to be able to sit and gaze upon the sun as it sets. When evening falls, take a moment to look up at the sky. Feel gratitude for having made it through another day. This moment will warm your spirit.

28

DON'T PUT OFF
WHAT YOU CAN DO TODAY.

You cannot regret the future.

Learn from a monk's last wishes.

At the end of Japan's Edo period (1603–1868), there was a famous monk and head priest named Sengai who lived in Hakata, on the western island of Kyushu.

When Sengai was near death, his disciples gathered to hear his last wishes. "I will not go with death," he said, meaning that he did not want to die. This, of course, did not conform to what might be expected of a Zen master's last wishes, so the disciples crept closer to his bedside and asked again for his final words.

He said, "Still, I will not go with death."

Even for this renowned priest, who took the tonsure at age eleven and dedicated himself to Zen spiritual training for the rest of his eighty-eight years—and who was presumed to have achieved enlightenment—there remained an attachment to this world.

One hundred percent of us will die—that is our fate as human beings. We know this, and yet in the face of death, we still cling to life. When I greet my own end, I will strive for as little attachment as I can. I would like to depart this world thinking that my life has been a good one.

I hope to embody the Zen concept that the way we live should complement our understanding of life and that we should strive to achieve the things of which we are capable.

29

DON'T THINK OF UNPLEASANT THINGS RIGHT BEFORE BED.

A five-minute "bed zazen"
before going to sleep

Time to reset your mind.

We all have nights when we cannot sleep, when we are troubled by unpleasant thoughts or plagued by anxieties or unable to alleviate our worries.

This is the perfect time to practice zazen.

The quiet practice of zazen releases in the brain the neurotransmitter serotonin, which functions as a mood stabilizer and has been shown to be effective in countering depression. Zazen can provide the therapeutic effect of boosting serotonin to the brain without the need to take medicine.

Once the brain is in a relaxed state, your blood vessels also gradually relax, improving your blood flow. This spreads warmth throughout your body.

With your mental haze cleared and your body warmed, you will naturally become sleepy.

When you get into bed, let go of whatever happened to you since waking up that morning, and be thankful for having made it through another day.

When you wake up the next morning, you will feel renewed. Do not underestimate the effects of five minutes of zazen before you go to sleep.

30

TRY YOUR BEST TO
DO WHAT YOU CAN NOW.

It will lead to good things.

Don't go chasing after clouds—you will never catch them.

There is a story about chasing clouds, and about clouds getting away.

You're out in the hot summer sun, working in the field. Without any clouds to shield the blazing sun, you must endure the heat. But then you look up at the sky, and off in the distance you spot a wisp of white.

"Ah, I bet it will be cooler in the shade of that cloud. I hope it makes its way over here soon," you think to yourself, and you even contemplate taking a break from your work until the cloud arrives.

But the reality is, the cloud may never arrive to protect you from the sun, and the day might end while you have paused your work, anticipating the shade.

Rather than wait for the cloud to approach, strive to do now what needs to be done. If you work intently, you may forget how hot it is. Then, before you know it, the cloud will arrive and bring with it a refreshing coolness.

What I'm talking about here could apply not only to clouds but also to fate or fortune. There's no point in envying someone else who has been blessed with a little luck. Nor does it do any good to lament your lack of opportunities. Simply work hard to do today what needs to be done. And fortune will surely come your way.

PART TWO

30 WAYS TO INSPIRE CONFIDENCE AND COURAGE FOR LIVING

Try changing your perspective.

31

DISCOVER ANOTHER YOU.

Find your inner protagonist.

*Your protagonist has
boundless potential.*

In order to live more freely, or with more ease, Zen Buddhism teaches the importance of not labeling ourselves as "this-or-that kind of person."

Let me give you an example.

There is another you within yourself. This version of you is freer than the self you think you know, and rich with potential. It is your essential self. Within yourself lives your true protagonist.

In Zen terms, the word for protagonist is also translated as "master." There is a famous story of a Zen monk who would address himself, saying, "Hey, master!" and his self would reply, "Yes?" He would then ask, "Are you awake?" and his self would again reply, "Yes!" He would continue this questioning in earnest.

Each of us plays various roles in society. You may be an office worker, a mother, or a cook in a restaurant. These are, without a doubt, our various "selves." But we each have another self, the true protagonist who lives within us.

Do your best to awaken this other self.

32

DON'T BE TROUBLED BY THINGS THAT HAVE NOT YET HAPPENED.

Anxiety is intangible.

Anxiety:
Where does it actually exist?

Zen Buddhism is said to have originated with a monk named Bodhidharma. He transmitted his teachings to a disciple named Huike.

One time, Huike shared his troubles with Bodhidharma.

"My mind is always filled with anxiety. Please help me to quiet it."

Bodhidharma replied, "I will calm these anxieties for you. But first, will you bring them to me? If you can set them before me and say, 'These are the anxieties that burden me,' I will be sure to calm them for you."

Hearing this, Huike realized something for the first time.

"Anxiety" was a thing within his mind. In reality, it was intangible.

His fears were intangible, and yet he clung to them. He recognized the futility in this.

There is no need to be troubled by things that have not yet happened. Think only about what is happening right now.

Almost all anxieties are intangible. They are the invention of your own mind.

33

TAKE PLEASURE IN YOUR WORK.

Work is what brings out
your inner protagonist.

Joy is to be found within yourself.

There is a teaching that a Rinzai Zen priest is said to have given his monks in training: "Be the master wherever you go. Then, wherever you find yourself, things will be as they truly are."

Always make every effort, no matter the circumstances or situation, to bring out your true self—your inner protagonist—to deal with whatever you face.

If we face everything in this manner, all of us will be capable of encountering the truth. And therein will we discover bliss. That is the meaning of this teaching.

When we have something arduous to do, we often want to complain about it. We say, "Anyone could do this," or "This is all they ever let me do." But with this attitude, it is very difficult to find the joy in our work.

People who do their best to enjoy what is before them have the greatest chance to discover inner peace. Often, whatever it is they are enjoying—the thing before them—has the potential to turn into an opportunity.

The place where you currently find yourself, the role you inhabit, the people you meet today, every little thing . . . you never know what might become an opportunity. Stop dismissing what it is that you're doing, and start living.

34

SIMPLY IMMERSE YOURSELF.

The tremendous power of being unfettered

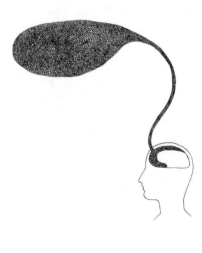

Empty your mind, and do not let it settle anywhere or wander.

There is a saying in Zen practice, *munen muso*, that describes a state of being free from worldly desires and distracting thoughts. Another way to say it is just *mushin*, or "clear mind." You empty your mind and do not let it settle anywhere or wander.

This allows you to focus on what needs to be done now, without worrying about all the other things in your life. It is a teaching that demonstrates the amazing power available to us if we can achieve a clear mind.

A Zen master named Takuan, from the Edo period [1603–1868], explained the secret of the Japanese form of fencing known as kendo in this way: "When you face another swordsman, if you think there is an opportunity to strike your opponent's shoulder, then your mind will be preoccupied by your opponent's shoulder. If you think there is an opportunity to strike his arm, then your mind will be preoccupied by his arm. If you think you can win against him, then your mind will be preoccupied by winning. Do not allow your mind to wander to or settle upon any of these places. Even as you focus your energy on a single point, keep your mind free and open. This is the secret of the sword."

Even when we think we are concentrating on our work, often we may be saying to ourselves, "How long until it's time for a break?" or "This work is so boring." And even when we are relaxing on a day off, thoughts about work may nag at us.

Try simply immersing yourself in what is before you. You may discover that doing so can be surprisingly powerful.

35

DO NOT FEEL PUT OUT BY THE TASKS BEFORE YOU.

A way to make work much more enjoyable

*"A day without working is
a day without eating."*

In Zen practice, we believe in the importance of not thinking about work as labor, and for this reason we call it *samu*.

When Buddhism first originated in India, monks did not engage in any form of productive activity—they lived solely on whatever alms they received. These offerings of food or money became known as *samu*.

However, when Buddhism spread to China, the temples were all built deep in the mountains. The monks were unable to descend from the mountains in order to beg for their keep, and so they began cultivating their own fields and growing crops—which became a form of practice. Work (*samu*) became the most important: If one didn't work, one couldn't eat. This is how we got the saying from the Zen master Baizhang Huaihai, "A day without working is a day without eating."

When we work every day, we tend to become occupied with the tasks before us, and with the attendant gains. But I believe that the essence of work is to be found in Baizhang's way of thinking.

In that sense, try to see your work as *samu*, or mindful work. Think of it as something that will nurture or educate you.

Only by thinking this way will you experience the true pleasure to be found in work.

36

DON'T BLAME OTHERS.

A way of thinking that will bring forth
opportunity and fortune

Think of the work you're doing
as an encounter.

At the office, there are people who produce results and people who seem never to be very effective. How can this be explained?

Human beings, for the most part, are endowed with basically the same capabilities.

So if there's anything that differentiates the results we produce, it may be the mind-set in which each of us faces whatever task is at hand.

Whatever it is you're doing, be grateful for the opportunity. Be happy for the chance to do the work. I don't mean to sound idealistic here—I'm merely repeating what many great men and women have said before.

If you believe that a task is being forced upon you, then you will see the work as a burden, and it will arouse negative feelings. It is the same in the practice of Zen. The moment you find yourself asking "Why do I have to tidy the garden every morning?" is the moment your training becomes meaningless.

Everything we do as human beings is precious. If we are to find meaning in what we do, we must first become our own protagonist in the work. You have the leading role in your work. If you approach work with this attitude, all work becomes meaningful and invaluable.

37

DON'T COMPARE
YOURSELF TO OTHERS.

When you feel as though
you're doing the wrong job

In anything,
the hard part is just to keep going.

"The work I'm doing now is my true calling." Whoever can say this is very fortunate.

Most people, though, are more likely to wonder, "Is this job really right for me? There must be other work that I'm better suited for."

Surely, people have their own aptitudes.

But there is something to be said for perseverance.

Practicing Zen monks wake early, sweep and purify the garden, perform religious services. . . . They repeat the same things every day, and the lesson is to be found in the repetition itself.

You can start something as long as you have the energy. Finishing, too, is easy. The hard part is just to keep going. If you tell yourself, day in and day out, that something is wrong for you, then how will it ever be right for you?

We have a tendency to compare ourselves to others. We envy the light workload of our neighbor. We see someone who is talented and get depressed. But, ultimately, there is pleasure to be found in the repetition of work that suits you.

38

SEEK NOT WHAT YOU LACK.

Be content with the here and now.

The quickest path to achieving results

There is a saying, "Summer fires and winter fans," which refers to untimely and useless things. But there will surely come a time when what is not immediately useful will be of use. I'm talking about the importance of waiting patiently for the right moment.

Although it might all be called work, some jobs may seem glamorous and enviable from the outside, and others unexciting and ordinary. All things being equal, it's human nature to want the glamorous job.

But for those who have a glamorous job, things weren't always glamorous. What you see now is the cumulative result of steadily working away at ordinary tasks.

What might now seem useless can turn out to be auspicious. Not a single effort goes to waste when you work hard in the present moment.

Your boss might ask, "Who can do this for me?" It's a boring assignment, and nobody raises their hand. But that is precisely the time to say, "I can do it."

Be the person who has that kind of attitude. It will be rewarded.

39

EVERY SO OFTEN,
TRY TO STOP THINKING.

Where ideas can be hiding

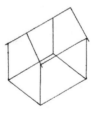

The benefits of having room in your mind

The empty state of not thinking about anything. It's not easy to achieve. Even practicing monks find it difficult.

But when you look back over your days, you find moments when you've achieved it unconsciously.

You look up at the sky and think, "Ah, what a beautiful cloud," and stare at it vacantly. Then you snap out of your reverie and say, "Hm, now what was I just thinking?"

I urge you to appreciate these moments.

At the office, when trying to solve a problem, everyone is frantic to hit on the right idea. You don't stop thinking for a moment; you just keep plugging away at it.

But when you want to come up with a good idea, this constant effort can be counterproductive.

Ideas or sparks actually emerge from the empty spaces within your mind—from the gaps between your thoughts.

To increase the chances of teasing out those ideas from between the gaps, cherish the time when you're not thinking about anything.

40

MAKE DISTINCTIONS.

The best way to relieve stress

Try erecting gates in your mind.

When we wake up in the morning, right away we turn on the computer and check our email or we read the news on our phone and look up the weather.

We live in a time of constant information, available anytime and anywhere. But in such a world, we have all the more reason to maintain proper on and off switches.

This is why distinctions are so important.

Try erecting gates in your mind.

For example, the grounds of your home constitute the first gate. When you leave home and cross this first gate, thoughts of work start to form in your head. The door of your car or the train is the second gate; once you cross it, you begin planning out your workday. And finally, when you arrive at your office and cross the third gate, you are ready to focus on your work.

When the workday is over and you arrive back at the first gate, it's important to leave work behind.

What's left is time to relax. To enjoy your home life.

This is surely the best way to relieve stress.

41

TRY ATTENDING A ZAZEN SITTING.

A chance to sweep the detritus
from your mind

*You can leave behind your stress
and worries at the temple.*

Many Zen temples now hold *zazenkai*, or zazen sittings open to the public.

Kenkoji, the temple where I am the resident priest, holds a weekly *zazenkai*. There's nothing challenging about it. Once you learn the fundamentals, anyone can do it.

We sit quietly in zazen and breathe from the abdomen. That is all it takes to warm the entire body, even in the cold of winter. When you breathe deeply, the blood flows all the way to your toes and you feel the warmth all over.

And recent research has shown that when you sit zazen, you enter an alpha state, with the brain waves associated with relaxation taking over.

People come to the temple burdened with thoughts and concerns. Then they sit quietly in zazen, during which time they calmly encounter their selves.

When they leave the temple, they also leave behind their worries.

The expression on their faces after they sit zazen is clear and serene. Every time I see this, it gives me tremendous pleasure.

Attending a *zazenkai* is an opportunity to sweep the detritus from your mind.

42

PLANT A SINGLE FLOWER.

*No day is more important
than today.*

In the world of nature,
every day is a new day.

Consider growing a single flower from a seed. Plant the seed in a pot. Talk to it every morning as you water it. In time, a small shoot will appear, and then a beautiful flower will bloom. The flower will grow—each day, each hour, each minute—and you will take notice of the changes.

In the world of nature, every day is a new day. As humans, we have a tendency to fixate on the past, but when you grow a flower from seed, you become aware that nothing and no one can remain in the same place.

A Zen lifestyle is one that is constantly in contact with nature. We perceive the life that dwells within nature and experience ourselves as part of it. A sense of well-being and peace of mind springs from that awareness.

Every morning, I walk through the temple garden. Although it's the same garden, it appears different from one day to the next. There are variations between sunny days and rainy days, and the number of fallen leaves fluctuates day by day. The garden is never the same from one day to the next.

We say, "Every day is new, and new again tomorrow."

It is the same for us as humans. The preoccupations of today will end today. Tomorrow there will be a new you. This is why there is no need to worry.

43

MAKE A PROPER START.

Create an "upward spiral."

How to generate lots of good around you

In Japan, when the new year begins, we pay our first visit to the shrine. There is a ceremony to pray for good fortune throughout the coming year.

Good fortune brings with it more good fortune. Misfortune attracts further misfortune. All the more reason to make a proper start.

This applies to work as well. For instance, you unexpectedly get a new job. If you make the most of this opportunity and throw yourself into the work with all you've got, it can lead to yet another job opportunity. If you appreciate good fortune when it first comes to you, it can bring a succession of more good fortune.

The opposite is true with misfortune. Once you take a step into misfortune, you can get caught in a downward spiral.

When you feel as though things aren't going well, try scolding yourself in a loud voice. In Zen, we use the word *katsu* as an exclamation to scold practitioners when they are struggling on the path to enlightenment. A well-timed *katsu* can turn the tide.

Cut off misfortune when it begins. And make sure to take advantage of good fortune. That is the secret to a good life.

44

CHERISH YOUR OWN SELF.

The meaning of carrying an amulet

An amulet is your alter ego.

I am sometimes asked the following questions by visitors to the temple:

"Master, what amulet is the most potent? Which one will have the greatest effect?"

People seem to have a misunderstanding about what an amulet is, and so I patiently explain it to them.

"Think of an amulet as an alter ego of the deity or of the Buddha himself. You're looking after the deity for a year. You must protect the deity. And by cherishing the amulet, you are cherishing your own self."

You may believe that by carrying an amulet, you can be a bit reckless with yourself, because the amulet will protect you. But you mustn't think this way. When you are reckless with your own self, you are putting in danger the deity as well.

In order to prevent this, always strive to be mindful of your behavior. Cherish your own self. That is the true meaning of carrying an amulet.

45

THINK SIMPLE.

*If you really want to
satisfy your mind*

*What might seem
deceptively appealing . . .*

Here is a story about something that happened to someone I know.

He had a craving for *omuraisu*, a dish of fried rice wrapped in an egg omelette and served with ketchup, so he went to a restaurant. As he was perusing the menu, what caught his eye was *hayashi-raisu*—hashed beef with rice. It was one of those menus with photos, and this item looked quite delicious. While he was debating which one to get, he noticed that they also offered *omu-hayashi*, a combination of these two dishes, and so he ordered this with glee.

He expected to be satisfied with this decision, but in the end, it didn't really taste like either dish. He would have been better off getting just one or the other.

This might sound like a silly story, but I think you can understand the message.

Namely, when you're uncertain, simplicity is the best way to go.

There is a Zen saying about samadhi, the state of intense concentration achieved through meditation: *Ichigyo zanmai.* It means "Strive for just one thing." Rather than branching out into this, that, and what-have-you, focus your attention on just one thing. This is the way to gain satisfaction and fulfillment. And, of course, if what you really crave is *omu-hayashi*, then that is the thing to get.

46

DO NOT FEAR CHANGE.

Cast off your attachment
to the past.

There is beauty to be found in change.

With the arrival of spring, the glory of the cherry blossoms in full bloom makes the heart leap.

The tightly closed buds open up, and then—in what seems like no time at all—the blossoms are at their peak. But in less than a week, the petals begin to fall, and all too soon the cherry trees are sprouting leaves. The brief scattering of petals is itself graceful. It is a constant and ever-changing scene. And the beauty of it all is captivating.

What the Japanese prize most is the fragility of the cherry blossoms' beauty. The blossoms are lovely because of their evanescence—we sense in them the ephemerality of life. It is said that this appreciation of the ephemeral is what enabled Zen Buddhism to take root and spread throughout Japan. There is, in fact, a deep connection between Zen thought and the reverence of cherry blossoms.

It is the same with our lives. Everything is constantly in flux. There are changes as we age and changes in our surroundings.

There is nothing to fear in these changes.

A supple mind accepts change and is not attached to the past. Rather than lament change, it finds new beauty and hope in it. That is a life to which to aspire.

47

NOTICE CHANGES.

*Everything else springs
from this awareness.*

The effect of observing yourself
from a fixed point

Practicing Zen monks generally rise every day at four in the morning. In Zen, we refer to wake-up time as *shinrei*, or "bell ringing," because it is announced with a handbell.

The monks wash up and then, at 4:15, they begin the morning zazen. We call this *kyoten*, or "dawn," zazen. Bedtime—*kaichin*, or "opening the pillow"—is at nine in the evening. We get seven hours of sleep. We lead a very regular lifestyle.

Why do Zen monks live this way?

To make them attuned to subtle changes in the mind and body.

When you maintain a regular lifestyle, you are able to notice the slightest changes. If you want to change yourself, first it is important to develop an awareness of any shifts within.

You might be able to do something today that you were unable to do yesterday. Your mood today may not be the same as it was yesterday. By making observations from a fixed point, you are able to see yourself as you really are. This is also how you can hone your mind and body, by taking good care of both.

Conscientious living begins with early to bed, early to rise.

This is the secret to a life of ease and contentment.

48

FEEL INSTEAD OF THINK.

To foster a true zest for life

The advantage of those who notice small changes

In earlier times, fishermen knew how to predict the weather without the use of modern-day forecasting. They used the direction of the wind or the look of the clouds. Without these skills, they could be putting their lives at risk.

They could also study the color of the water or the behavior of birds to figure out where the fish would be. They dedicated themselves to honing all of their senses in order to guarantee their safety and to catch the fish they needed for their livelihood.

When resourcefulness like this yields results, it can be very satisfying.

I believe in the importance of honing the five senses in order to experience such satisfaction. It is one of life's pleasures.

Try picking up a stone by the side of the road. Touch it, and notice what it smells like. Stones have a front and a back, each with a different feel. You may think that stones have no scent, but mountain stones smell like the mountains, and sea stones smell like the sea. Details like these are all around you. Take an interest in them, using your senses to notice variations in nature.

Hone your senses so that you won't miss even the slightest changes.

49

DON'T LET THINGS GO TO WASTE.

For instance, try eating radish greens.

What is a "Zen mind"?

If I were to describe a Zen mind in just a few words, I would say it is about making good use of everything.

For example, when preparing meals, there is almost nothing we throw away. Take the leaves of a daikon radish: Most people just toss them in the garbage, but if you pickle them, they make a delicious side dish.

We also never throw out leftovers. If we realize we won't be able to finish our portion, we are quick to offer it to someone else.

This kind of practice adds a beautiful polish to the mind.

The essence of Zen is in the beauty of simple things. There is beauty to be found in things that are stripped of everything that is unnecessary and that are without ornamentation. In a building, for example, beauty might be found in the structure or the raw materials. Needless ornamentation would destroy its essential beauty. This is how we see things.

Appreciate the basic materials or ingredients, no matter what they are.

It is a simple way to hone both your mind and your lifestyle.

50

DON'T BE BOUND BY A SINGLE PERSPECTIVE.

*There is more than just
"the proper way."*

The concept of mitate

In Japanese, we talk about the concept of *mitate*—seeing a certain item not in its originally intended form but as another thing; seeing something as resembling something else and putting it to use in another way. The notion of *mitate* originates in the aesthetics of the tea ceremony, in which practitioners put everyday objects to use in elevated forms—for example, a gourd that was originally a water flask being used as a flower vase.

Utensils age after years of use. An item's utility becomes obsolete. But that does not necessarily mean the end of its life. You can discover a different use for it and breathe new life into the object itself. This spirit is at the heart of Zen.

Take, for instance, a millstone. Over years of use, it becomes abraded and grains can no longer be ground on it. But this does not mean the end of its life. It could be set out in the garden, perhaps used as a stepping-stone. Or a teacup that has a chipped rim might now be used as a bud vase.

Objects do not have merely one purpose. They can be used in myriad ways, depending upon the user's imagination. How will you use an object? That is the aesthetic concept of *mitate*.

There is abundance not in the accumulation of things, but in knowing how to use things well.

Try seeing things in different ways, so as not to be bound by just "the proper way."

51

THINK WITH YOUR OWN HEAD.

Be skeptical of common sense.

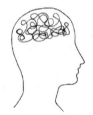

*Knowledge and wisdom are similar
but not the same.*

Knowledge and wisdom—they may appear to be the same, but they are not.

Things you learn either in school or on your own—this is knowledge.

Wisdom, on the other hand, is what you know from actually putting these things to use.

Both knowledge and wisdom are important for living a happy life. You mustn't privilege one over the other. Keep them in balance.

The Zen monk Ikkyu, famous for his wit, often demonstrated how keen both his knowledge and his wisdom were through the brilliant ways he solved difficult problems. In my opinion, people who possess enough knowledge to know how to apply it in particular situations are able to move nimbly through life.

In today's world, when we're constantly inundated with information, there is a tendency to neglect using our own brains to think. It can often seem we're about to burst with knowledge.

But how you live your life is your own decision. And this is all the more reason to have wisdom—to help you decide how to go about your life once you've acquainted yourself with the various ways there are to live.

See as much as you can. Feel as much as you can. And make sure to think with your own head.

52

BELIEVE IN YOURSELF.

When you give up,
your potential drops to zero.

Possibility springs from confidence.

In Zen we say, "All things come from nothingness." These words apply especially to human nature.

We are all born naked. That is, without any possessions. Absolutely nothing.

Looking at it another way, you could also say that it is precisely when we have nothing that our potential is unlimited. And it is within this nothingness that we can find infinite possibilities. Or as we say in Zen, "Within nothingness there is infinite potential."

There is capability within all of us—no one has zero potential.

The question is, how do we unleash it?

For those who feel stuck, or that they have lost their conviction, the answer is to boost your belief in yourself.

Your capabilities have yet to be fully realized. If you make an effort to unleash more of your potential, you will see a breakthrough. You will believe in the possibilities within yourself.

Life doesn't always go smoothly. Our efforts sometimes go unrewarded. Despite this, try to believe in yourself and do your best. Do not fear moving forward.

53

INSTEAD OF WORRYING,
GET MOVING.

A much easier way to
meet a challenge

For those who plant
the seeds of their own anxiety

I teach at a university, and students often consult me about finding a job.

I hear things like, "Even if I apply to a company I really like, I may not get a response," or "When I look at the employment stats for this company, it seems like they don't take many recruits from our university." A lot of these students feel like giving up.

I tell them, "Don't worry so much about the numbers. Get out there and see for yourself."

Whether you're worried about jobs or interpersonal relationships, if you keep everything in your head, you just allow feelings like "I can't do this" or "That'll never work" to take hold.

But if you leap into it with both feet, you may be surprised by how easy it is to accomplish something or to come up with a solution. Just like with bungee jumping or riding a roller coaster, the scariest part is not the doing but the moment right before it.

Be honest: Do you plant the seeds of your own anxiety?

It's a waste of time to get lost in a labyrinth of your own making.

Instead, direct your energies to the reality you're facing and take one step at a time.

54

MAINTAIN A SUPPLE MIND.

What purpose does hard work serve?

A supple mind is a strong mind.

When someone criticizes us, we immediately feel wounded. When something unpleasant happens, we cannot get it out of our head. What can we do to bounce back?

One way to strengthen the mind is through cleaning.

When we clean, we use both our head and our body. While what we learn from expending mental effort may be important, what our body learns from physical labor has a greater effect on mental strength.

The practice of Zen Buddhism involves learning through physical labor. Zen monks wake up early in the morning and clean. When it's cold out, sweeping and wiping down everything with a damp cloth is difficult for anyone. But once we've finished, the moment we step into that neat and tidy space we feel refreshed. You cannot experience this unless you have cleaned it yourself.

Hard work and perseverance. Some people frown whenever they hear these words.

You may be wondering, "What purpose do they serve?" They serve your own.

When we work hard with our head, heart, and body, we cannot help but grow stronger. We become better equipped to respond to life with a supple mind.

55

GET ACTIVE.

Become more down-to-earth.

*Some things you can appreciate only when
you do them yourself.*

We have a saying in Zen: "Experience for yourself hot and cold." It means that no matter how you try to explain the coolness or warmth of, for example, water, you cannot really know it without touching it. It's about the importance of first-hand experience.

There is a television personality in Japan named Miyoko Omomo. She paid a visit to her hometown in Niigata after it had been transformed by the 2004 Chuetsu earthquake, and she wondered what she could do to help. Having been born into a family of farmers, she rented a plot of land and started cultivating rice on it herself. During the week she would do her job in Tokyo, and on weekends she would return to her hometown to work in the fields. She did every task herself, from weeding to harvesting, and didn't hesitate to get her hands dirty.

I heard her talking about it on a radio program: "I had never tasted more delicious rice. It was as if I could see the face of the Kannon (the goddess of mercy) in every single grain."

She was able to appreciate the significance of the rice that she herself had worked hard to cultivate and harvest. She had literally gotten "down to earth."

There are some things you can appreciate only when you do them yourself.

56

WAIT FOR THE
RIGHT OPPORTUNITY.

When things don't go the way you want

The Japanese mind-set

Historically, the Japanese have been an agricultural people. We till the land, and we live by the grace of nature's bounty.

The culture of an agricultural people is, as it were, a forest culture. Unlike in the desert, there is an abundance of food in the forest. The trees produce flowers and bear fruit, nuts, and berries. Not knowing when the trees' offerings would fall, our ancestors gathered beneath the trees and waited. Thus developed a culture of gathering.

After eating the fallen fruit, they would plant the seeds in the soil. Sprouts would appear, and there would be enough so that there was no need to steal others' bounty.

You might say that because of this heritage, Japanese people are innately calm and have a mind-set of waiting for the right opportunity and of helping one another.

Observe nature attentively. Open your ears to nature's voice and get accustomed to its rhythm. This can lead to deep contemplation, which can help to make it apparent what should be done next.

When work or interpersonal relationships aren't going well, throwing yourself into finding a solution is one possibility.

But there are times when waiting for the right moment can be better.

57

APPRECIATE YOUR
CONNECTION WITH THINGS.

*Recognize the luxury of
not having things.*

*An appreciation for things is an
appreciation for yourself.*

Even though you already have a computer, when the latest model is released, suddenly you want it. Although you've had your car for only three years, you're eager to replace it with a newer one. Desire feeds upon itself, and the mind becomes dominated by boundless greed. This is not happiness.

Consider the things that surround you now. Develop an appreciation for them. There is something specific that connects you with them, a reason why you acquired them. Take good care of them; treat them like they are the best things.

You may decide you want a car, and then work hard to save money for it. There's nothing wrong with that. The important thing is to treat it with love once you have it.

Think of the things that are connected to you as parts of yourself. It's rare to find someone who does not care about herself; once you acquire something and begin to take care of it, a love for it will spring up. What is most important is your attitude toward the things that belong to you.

Use the same things for years, even for decades. You will feel good about the time spent with them. Think about the connection between people and things. Treat both well, as you would yourself.

58

TRY JUST SITTING QUIETLY IN NATURE.

Make time to look closely at yourself.

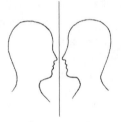

*The reason why,
when you encounter a garden, you have
an unconscious desire to sit down.*

The temples in Kyoto and Nara attract many visitors. Their gardens have existed for hundreds of years. When we see these gardens, we automatically find ourselves sitting down. Although we can view them while standing or walking, for some reason we find that we want to sit. Sitting encourages contemplation.

What we think about will differ from person to person, but when we encounter a garden, some of us may reflect upon the garden itself. By doing so, we transcend hundreds of years and are able to enjoy a quiet dialogue with the people who created it.

Within the relaxed flow of a contemplative state, we try to discover our own existence. It presents an opportunity to re-examine our everyday self.

It is very important to make time for this kind of experience. You need not go all the way to Kyoto or Nara—a garden, temple, or church in your neighborhood will do just as well.

Try sitting and having a dialogue with nature.

59

TRY CLEARING YOUR HEAD.

*Become aware of which
senses are being stimulated.*

Do less, not more

By emptying our mind, we enable a state of nothingness. In the world of Zen, we call this *mushiryo*, or "beyond thinking." It refers to a state in which we retain nothing within ourselves.

Clear your head and look up at the sky—you will see the shifting clouds. Empty your mind and listen actively—all around you are the various interwoven sounds of nature: the singing of small birds, the wind rustling fallen leaves.

Even if you're in a city, there are still many sounds and scenes that evoke nature. Take in as much of this natural world as you can. By doing so, you will notice that you, too, are a part of nature.

For example, the rain that falls from the clouds you saw up in the sky empties into a river or becomes groundwater that eventually will be your drinking water. This is the moment when you experience the full interconnectedness of nature.

Especially when you're busy, make time to clear your head.

Even for just a few short minutes, try the Zen practice of *mushiryo*, of going beyond thinking and nonthinking. You may be surprised by how much it can calm your mind and suffuse your entire body with tremendous power.

60

ENJOY A ZEN GARDEN.

*Experience how such a garden is
imbued with the "Zen mind."*

There are healing powers within
a Zen garden.

Visiting an ancient city in Japan gives us the opportunity to appreciate the gardens of Zen temples.

In a literal sense, all the gardens on the grounds of Zen Buddhist temples can be considered Zen gardens.

But this is not really the case.

Why? Take, for instance, Zen painting.

Let's consider a *sumi-e* ink painting of Bodhidharma done by a famous Japanese painter. No matter how splendid a painting it might be, we would not call it a Zen painting.

What I mean to say is that both Zen gardens and Zen paintings adhere to a specific form. They are definitive expressions of the creator's mastery of a Zen state, which is also called Buddha mind.

One trains in Zen Buddhism for a long time before one achieves Buddha mind. In that Zen state, the unique beauty of one's imagined landscape can be expressed in a Zen garden or painting. It conveys an ease that can heal the mind.

Instead of just seeing the superficial beauty of a Zen garden, try to experience the Zen mind that it is imbued with. Once you feel integrated into the garden, you will not even notice the passage of time. The more you appreciate the concepts that permeate the garden, the more it can heal your mind.

PART THREE

20 WAYS TO ALLEVIATE CONFUSION AND WORRY

Try changing how you interact with others.

61

SERVE PEOPLE.

The starting point
for a contented life

Where does worry come from?

A state of utter clarity, uncomplicated by desire or any attachments—that is the state of "nothingness," which Zen emphasizes above all else.

This emptiness of thought is the basis for the teachings of the Buddha, and for his fundamental notions of impermanence and insubstantiality. The Buddha teaches that human suffering occurs when we lack awareness of this impermanence and insubstantiality.

In other words, our confusion and worry stem from an inability to accept that the world is constantly changing, from a belief—or an unconscious hope—that our selves and our possessions, as well as the people who surround us, will never change.

It is precisely when we are betrayed by such a hope that we experience distress.

Everything exerts an influence on everything else.

For example, if you decide that you want to be happy, you need for the people around you to be happy as well. This is how serving others can help to bring about your own happiness.

Do not cling to your belief in what is and always should be. Practice nonattachment. By doing so, you will be serving the happiness of others.

Bear this in mind, and you will have a much more contented life.

62

CAST AWAY THE
"THREE POISONS."

*Bring a Zen mind-set
into your life.*

卌

*Keep your desires and anger in check, and
strive to understand the nature of things.*

In Buddhism, there are what we call the "three poisons." These
are not the kind of poisons that you can ingest; the teachings
refer to them as passions or worldly desires. They are the root
of human suffering, and they prevent us from attaining enlightenment.

The three poisons are greed, anger, and ignorance.

When we are afflicted with greed, once we acquire whatever it is we desire, we are still left wanting more. Anger
makes us enraged by the slightest things, and once it is pro-
voked, we take it out on others. Ignorance is a state of foolish-
ness: We are heedless of common sense or knowledge, and
lacking in education—but actually lacking an understanding
of our true Buddha nature.

As long as we allow ourselves to be governed by these
three poisons, we will be unable to find peace.

In contrast, the teachings say, if we can cast away these
three poisons, or worldly afflictions, we can live happily and
freely.

Whenever you notice any of the three poisons begin to
show themselves, try to calm your mind by regulating your
breathing. This can stop the afflictions from taking hold.

63

CULTIVATE YOUR SENSE OF GRATITUDE.

The deeper meaning of
a casual phrase

*A few simple words that
are full of warmth.*

When someone asks, "How are you?" we reply, in Japanese, *Okagesama de*, or "Everything is fine, thank God."

This happens all the time, but it is a lovely and, I think, very Japanese exchange.

A person cannot live by his or her good graces alone. We require the support of others, and we get by thanks to them. Obvious as this may seem, we still tend to forget. And the more we tend to forget, the more we ought to convey these sentiments in words.

"Good morning" in Japanese is *Ohayo gozaimasu*, which literally means "It is early." Implicit in this expression is, "It is early in the day, and having made it safely thus far, let's continue to strive for the best."

Another common Japanese phrase is *itadakimasu*, which we say before eating. It is an expression of gratitude toward the food we are about to enjoy. It also conveys gratitude toward the people who made the food for us. Whether it be fish or vegetables, the food still contains life. By consuming this life, we ourselves are sustained and are able to go on living. For this we are very grateful. All of these sentiments are contained within the expression *itadakimasu*.

These common phrases may seem so familiar as to be automatic, but they carry deep reserves of meaning and feeling.

64

DEMONSTRATE, RATHER THAN ASSERT, HOW YOU FEEL.

*The way to convey your
true intentions*

Understand the thinking behind
uchimizu, *the Japanese practice of*
sprinkling water outside a gate.

Express how you feel casually and without saying a word, rather than spelling it out. When it comes to conveying your true intentions, actions speak louder than words.

On a hot summer day, you may be expecting someone to visit.

Before they arrive, sprinkle water outside the gate. This act of sprinkling water serves to purify the entrance to your home and to make your guest feel welcome. The visitor sees the unevaporated water on the sidewalk, or the droplets on the flowers, and thinks, "Oh, they are expecting me. How hospitable!"

There's absolutely nothing pushy or imposing about this. It's merely a gracious welcome and a beautiful gesture that is uniquely Japanese.

When it comes to conveying your wishes or intentions, there is no wisdom in being insistent or assertive.

The Japanese have always had a sixth sense for interpreting sentiment, whether by tuning in to others or by tacit understanding.

We communicate with others with every breath we take, and without forgetting our heart's nature.

65

EXPRESS YOUR MIND,
BUT NOT IN WORDS.

What you can see
is not all there is.

Why are Zen paintings done in ink?

Zen philosophy holds the following to be true: "Spiritual awakening is transmitted outside of the sutras. It cannot be experienced through words or letters."

What this means is that the essence of Zen teaching cannot be put into words—neither written nor spoken.

Zen painting is an example of this.

Multiple colors are not used in Zen painting—only the single hue of the ink. The reason? It is believed that true beauty cannot be expressed through colors and that colors are an imperfect expression of the ineffability of beauty. And so colors are avoided.

Each of us experiences the splendor of the setting sun differently. Even if we all describe the color as crimson, we might each perceive that color in a different way. By using only ink, the painter allows every viewer to experience the crimson of the sunset however they like.

This is why it is said that Zen painting uses ink to express all five colors—green, blue, yellow, purple, and red.

An infinite range of colors can be found within ink's hue. Depending on the viewer, the ink takes on various tints and layers. What you can see is not all there is.

66

FOCUS ON OTHERS' MERITS.

*Especially when their faults
are on display*

In both gardens and interpersonal relationships, what is paramount is harmony.

Japanese gardens are not designed by cutting and pasting various components onto the landscape. The whole garden is composed in a way that makes the most of each element's particular features, such as the shape of a rock or how a certain tree bends.

What does it mean to make the most of an element in a garden?

Let's say that a garden will have several trees in it. We cannot simply plant the trees and be done with it. It's important to identify the ideal shape of each tree.

What kind of mood does this particular tree have? How should we plant this tree—in which position, and facing in which direction—in order to bring out its most attractive qualities?

In other words, we must appreciate the individuality of every tree and then coax it into expression. By understanding a tree's essence, we can bring it into harmony with the other elements of the garden.

The same goes for relationships among people.

We must recognize the individuality of ourselves and of others in order to get along. This is not to say that you must adapt to someone else, but by focusing on others' merits, you can create a beautiful relationship.

67

DEEPEN YOUR CONNECTION WITH SOMEONE.

The true meaning of
"once in a lifetime"

.

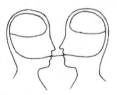

Concentrate on a single encounter.

It seems that nowadays, people care only about superficial relationships. The wider their range of acquaintances, the better. Networking is key. In the business world, of course, this is very important.

But in your personal life, it doesn't matter if your circle of friends is small. I don't expect there to be many people whom I can confide in. It is more enriching to build one meaningful relationship than to amass one hundred insubstantial connections. At least that's my opinion.

There is a saying that originates in Zen: *ichi-go ichi-e*, or "once in a lifetime." It means that we should treasure each and every encounter, because we may meet a person only once in our lifetime.

This is not to suggest that we should increase the number of encounters we have or that we should have more friends. Concentrate on a single encounter, and build a meaningful relationship. What's important is not the number of your connections but their depth.

68

FINE-TUNE YOUR TIMING.

This applies just as well to
interpersonal relationships.

Don't be too rushed or too relaxed.

There is a saying in Japanese, *sottaku doji*, which means, literally, "pecking simultaneously from the inside and out."

It is used to describe what happens when a chick is hatching from its egg: The first part refers to the chick and its pecking from inside the shell; the second part, to the response of the parent bird when it hears the chick and it pecks to help the chick emerge.

This is a very delicate situation. If the parent breaks the shell before the chick is fully formed, the chick will die. So the parent must listen very closely to the sound of the pecking from the inside and decide when it's safe to add its own careful pecking from the outside to help break the shell.

In other words, *sottaku doji* is about finding the perfect timing for both of them.

It's obvious how this relates to raising children, but it also has other applications.

When training someone at work, you cannot rush them or be too relaxed. And when you're being trained, it's your responsibility to send a signal that you're ready to progress.

The best results come from both parties having the right timing and being in sync.

69

GIVE UP THE NEED TO BE LIKED BY EVERYONE.

This is true even for Zen monks.

Don't get caught up; don't be biased;
don't be too fussy.

Interpersonal relationships can be complicated. No matter how hard you try, it's difficult to be open-minded toward everybody. Even monks at a Zen temple do not always get along.

There's no need to tell yourself, "I'm going to try to get in good with this person," or "I'm going to get to know this person better." Being attached to the notion of getting along or being friends with someone will hinder you. You will get caught up with not wanting to be disliked. This only creates tension.

Don't get caught up; don't be biased; don't be too fussy. Why not let go of trivial attachments and be more laid-back? I'm not suggesting that you try to be unpopular, but by the same token, don't try too hard to be well liked.

When a flower blooms, the butterfly naturally finds it. When trees have blossomed, birds flock to the branches on their own, and when the leaves wither and fall, the birds scatter.

Relationships with people aren't so different.

70

DON'T FIXATE ON
RIGHT AND WRONG.

This is about compromise.

If you fuss over black and white,
you miss out on the beauty of gray.

Buddhism is an extremely tolerant religion.

Buddhists don't think in terms of black and white. Some things are white, some are black, and in between are various shades of gray. This broad-minded spirit is at the heart of Buddhism, and it has a lot to do with how it took root in Japan.

Shinto has been practiced in Japan since ancient times, and at some point Buddhism arrived from China. Instead of pitting Shinto against Buddhism, the Japanese thought that somehow these two religions could coexist.

The Japanese concept of *honji suijaku* holds that Shinto gods are manifestations of Buddhist deities, and together they form an indivisible whole sanctified at local Shinto shrines in what is called *gongen*.

This may seem perfectly noncommittal, but that's exactly why it's an excellent example of Japanese wisdom. It's a way for both sides to coexist, by finding a compromise and avoiding conflict.

Things don't need to be defined as right or wrong, black or white.

Instead of coming down on one side or the other, a compromise may be the best way.

71

SEE THINGS
FOR WHAT THEY ARE.

*Hatred and affection share
the same true nature.*

The best way to avoid
like or dislike

Office relationships are apt to be difficult. Someone may say, "It's all my subordinate's fault," or "If only he weren't my boss." We may think we'd be better off if we'd never met some of our colleagues, but when these are people we work with, we have no choice.

Difficulties in interpersonal relationships—you could say that this is an eternal theme.

Muso Kokushi, who is known as "the father of Zen gardens," once said the following:

"The central benefit of Zen, in the context of the ordinary ups and downs of life, is not in preventing the minus and promoting the plus but in directing people to the fundamental reality that is not under the sway of ups and downs." This could mean, for example, that by holding a memorial service for your sworn enemy, or by confessing your own actions, you can turn a bad deed into a good one.

In other words, both misfortune and good fortune share the same origin. Hatred and affection are, in fact, one and the same.

Then what is their true nature? To put it succinctly, it is your own mind. Our preferences, our likes and dislikes—everything is a product of our own mind. In Zen Buddhism we say, "When you reach enlightenment, there are no likes or dislikes." When we can see things for what they are, our predilections disappear.

72

SKILLFULLY DETACH.

"Pay no attention"
is also Buddhist wisdom.

*"Unmoved even when
the eight winds blow."*

Words are important.

But it is more important not to be swayed by words.

At work or in social situations, there may be times when we find ourselves hurt by words that are directed at us. Even though someone may intend to be encouraging, the person on the receiving end can hear their words as cruel or harsh. A single word from a colleague can pierce like a dagger.

But negative comments should quickly be forgotten. This can be done by skillfully "paying no attention."

The Zen mind is said to be "unmoved even when the eight winds blow." We strive to remain unperturbed, no matter the situation—and even to be calm and good-humored.

Try freeing yourself from attachment to things. Do not be attached to words, either. Even when your interactions with someone are strained, do not be attached to the relationship. Try putting it at a distance.

This is the wisdom of the Buddha.

To live freely, we must acquire an unfettered mind.

73

DO NOT THINK IN TERMS OF LOSS AND GAIN.

Where does the awareness of our weaknesses come from?

People we get along well with,
and those we don't

We cannot help but have weaknesses. Someone may not mean any harm or offense, but because of their words or actions, we end up annoyed or with hurt feelings. Most likely you know someone who has this effect on you.

How do these people seem to know how to get to us?

Let me explain briefly the concept of *ishiki*, or "mental consciousness," within Zen thought.

You meet someone for the first time and think, "Oh, she seems nice," or "It seems like I might hit it off with him." This relates to the *i*, the first character of *ishiki*, which corresponds to the mind or the heart.

But what about the second character, the *shiki*? This is about making a judgment of someone's value. "That person could be useful to my career," or "This guy will get me nowhere." The more we do this, the more our weaknesses are revealed.

One hundred people will have one hundred different ways of reasoning or making judgments. Instead of having a gain-or-loss mentality and thinking in terms of whether someone is useful, consider someone's suitability or compatibility. Doing so will relieve a lot of the pressure on your relationships.

74

DO NOT GET CAUGHT UP
WITH MERE WORDS.

*The importance of
reading others' feelings*

Consider what others say
with empathy.

People's feelings cannot always be expressed in words. Some people may not have an easy time describing how they feel.

This is why we have the ability to read other people's feelings.

There is a Zen saying, *Nenge misho.* This refers to a riddle about the Buddha, known as a koan. From his dharma seat before his many disciples, the Buddha is said to have not uttered a word, but merely twirled a single flower in his hand and given a subtle smile. The disciples were mystified, and among those present, Mahakashyapa was the only one who returned the Buddha's smile. Mahakashyapa understood the Buddha's wordless gesture and, having received this dharma transmission, was designated as his successor.

It is still important, of course, to try to express our feelings in words. And conversely, we must pay close attention to what other people say.

But we mustn't lose sight of what is most essential by getting caught up in mere words. We should not only listen to what others have to say, but also consider their feelings with empathy.

75

DO NOT BE SWAYED BY THE OPINIONS OF OTHERS.

The secret to breaking free from confusion

Decisiveness is about having the ability to trust in yourself.

The arrangement of rocks plays a central role in Zen gardens. Rocks can be configured in endless ways, to represent microcosms, symbolizations, and abstractions. In my work as a garden designer and practicing Zen monk, you might say that my designs correspond to the state of my mind. This is why there is such a positive tension among the elements in Zen gardens.

The actual work I do is not something I can manage on my own. Large rocks and trees must be transported. Various tools are necessary, and the work itself requires a team.

Before completing a Zen garden, I need to borrow the hands of many.

In my experience, however, if I focus too much on what the team sees, then it can be difficult to complete the garden as an expression of my own thoughts.

Although it may seem counterintuitive, when it comes to coordinating what direction the rocks will face, the fewer people involved, the easier it is to synchronize.

And when it's time to make the final adjustments, it's best to do it alone.

Decisiveness is about having the ability to trust in yourself.

76

HAVE FAITH.

Benefit from the wisdom
of your elders.

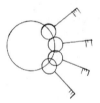

*Find the keys to life in
the stories of older people.*

Those who possess what is known as faith, or the core of how to live, are never the least bit discouraged. This is absolutely beyond a doubt.

But how do you come to have faith?

You can learn from the mentors around you.

There are quite a number of skills that you can acquire from studying older people, who are your great mentors in everything. Whether it's stories of their successes or of their failures, it can be very beneficial to listen to what they have to say.

Look around you—there are probably plenty of older people in your orbit. Each of them has her own life story. And each has her own experience and knowledge—which is exponentially greater than what you've learned in life so far. Such a wonderful resource, so close at hand.

The stories older people have to tell about everything they've seen and experienced are invaluable. Unlike the knowledge that is to be found in books or in school, this is firsthand experience, straight from the heart and lived in the flesh. Here in their true stories you can find the keys to life.

77

HAVE A CONVERSATION
WITH A GARDEN.

The things you miss when you are
caught up in appearances

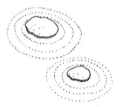

The meaning of
wabi-sabi

A Zen monk will go into the mountains to devote himself to Buddhist training. While engaged in his practice, deep in the mountains and far from any village, he might receive a visitor.

"I sincerely regret bringing you all the way here, to the middle of nowhere," he might apologize to the visitor. This apology—in Japanese, *wabi*—is the first component of the Japanese aesthetic of *wabi-sabi*.

The second part—the *sabi*—refers to a similar sentiment: "Thank you for coming all the way to such a lonely and remote place." *Sabi* is also a homonym that connotes patina or rust—the beauty that comes with age—and likely reflects the monk's humble abode. It evokes the monk's loneliness, or, in Japanese, *sabishii*.

All of which is to say that the spirit of *wabi-sabi* is grounded in a consideration for others. This sentiment is also to be found in Zen gardens.

When designing a Zen garden, the placement of the rocks or the arrangement of the sand is not the first consideration. Initially it is not about a specific shape or appearance, but rather the sentiment that the garden should embody.

Try having a conversation with a Zen garden. Experience the melancholy beauty that the garden designer was trying to convey, and respond to it in your own way.

78

MAKE SOMEONE HAPPY.

Something to enhance your meals

*Japanese hospitality can evoke the flow of
time, even at the dining table.*

When entertaining guests, you might treat them to a multi-course meal, featuring special, high-quality ingredients—a Western feast.

Japanese hospitality is a bit different. Above all, the Japanese prize cuisine that demonstrates an awareness of the season.

The choice of what to serve is determined by what is perfectly in season at the time. And there are two other elements: a trace of something that is just past its season, evoking the departing moment, and something that is just now coming into season, suggesting an impending arrival.

In other words, the meal includes the last of the previous season, the height of the current season, and the first of the coming season. These three things conjure the flow of time— the past, the present, and the future—for the guest's enjoyment.

The height of hospitality is not necessarily attained with the most sophisticated ingredients. Whether it is with a meal you prepare or a gift you give, try incorporating a sense of the flow of time to make your guests happy.

79

FIND OCCASIONS TO
GET TOGETHER WITH FAMILY.

Where you can show up as you are

Becoming aware of
what's really important

Just what does it mean to have a family?

People marry, they raise children, they live together—but this is just how it looks from the outside.

It is among family where we can find true peace of mind, a place for emotional support.

When we're among family, we don't have to try so hard or keep up appearances—we can just be who we are. You could say that a Zen lifestyle strives for the same thing. It might seem simple, but it's actually quite difficult. We all want to hide our weaknesses and portray ourselves as more or better than we are.

But when we live this way, eventually it catches up to us. This is exactly why we need family—where we can let our real self be seen.

Even if you don't live near your family, the next time you visit them, take the time to sit and talk with them.

The place where you can show up as you are. Time spent there can heal a weary mind and revitalize your heart.

80

APPRECIATE ALL THE PEOPLE
WHO CAME BEFORE YOU.

*Realizing the miracle of
"being here now"*

If you were to take away just one of your ancestors, you wouldn't exist.

Japanese people used to have large families. There was the grandfather and grandmother, then the parents, then the children. Three or four generations, all living together under one roof—this facilitated the passing down of family history.

The eighty-year-old grandfather might tell his five-year-old grandchild about his own grandfather. The grandchild could hear stories from two hundred years earlier. He would know what kind of people his ancestors were. This makes history truly come alive.

It is thanks to the existence of your ancestors that you are here today. If you go back ten generations, you might find more than a thousand ancestors. Imagine how many more there would be if you were to go back twenty generations, or even thirty—it could be more than a million people. And if you were to take away just a single one of these ancestors, you would not have been born.

When you think about it this way, you cannot help but feel a sense of gratitude to your ancestors. It genuinely seems like a miracle that you are here. When we become aware of this miracle, we come to understand the preciousness of life.

PART FOUR

20 WAYS TO MAKE ANY DAY THE BEST DAY

Try shifting your attention to the present moment.

81

BE HERE NOW.

The you of a moment ago
is the past you.

Focus on the here and now
rather than on the past.

As humans, we live only in the moment, in the here and now. So we must train our mind to be present in this very instant. This is the Zen way of thinking.

Zen Buddhists like to say, "Dwell in the three worlds." These three worlds are the past, the present, and the future. In Zen Buddhism, you often hear the names Amida, Shaka (Shakyamuni), and Miroku; these represent the Buddha in each of the three worlds.

If you are wondering how this way of thinking actually works, let's start with our breathing. We inhale, and then we exhale. The moment when we inhale is the present, but once we exhale, it has already become the past. To put it another way, when you were reading the preceding pages in this book, that was the you of the past. And when you read the following pages, that will be the you of the future.

When something bad happens and you are feeling down, try clapping your hands in front of you—in an instant you can feel better, having been put in a new frame of mind. Like when a movie cuts to a new scene, there is now a totally different you.

What is important is this day, this hour, this moment.

82

BE GRATEFUL FOR EVERY DAY,
EVEN THE MOST ORDINARY.

*The happiness to be found
in the unremarkable*

*The greatest happiness is in the
natural order of things.*

The Zen monk Ikkyu, famous for his wit, was once asked by a merchant celebrating the birth of his grandchild to write something congratulatory. Ikkyu thought for a moment, and then wrote, "The parent dies, the child dies, the grandchild dies." The merchant read it with a puzzled expression, then complained, "Why have you written something so morbid?"

Here is what Ikkyu said.

"First the parent dies, then the child dies, and at last the grandchild grows old and dies. That is the natural order. If your family is able to experience death in the natural order, you will have the greatest happiness." Everyone could not help but agree.

To make it through today, another uneventful and ordinary day.

To breathe in and out, to do our work, to sleep well.

Ordinary and unremarkable as it may seem, this is actually what makes it all the more amazing.

The simple happiness of the passage of one day after another—such happiness is right before our eyes.

83

RECOGNIZE THAT
YOU ARE PROTECTED.

We are all
in the palm of the Buddha.

So take heart and keep going!

In the Buddhist way of thought, it is said that all of us are in the palm of the Buddha. No matter how much we struggle, in the end we're just flailing around in his hand.

You might hear this and think, "Then why not just give up?" Quite the opposite.

There will be things that don't go as expected, and you may feel miserable, but ultimately you are protected, as I said, in the palm of the Buddha. That is why you should take heart and keep going!

All of us are on our own in life. And yet despite this aloneness, the Buddha sees everything we do. This should be a balm—it should enliven our spirit. The Buddha is all-seeing—he sees the good as well as the bad. Belief in this propels us forward.

The existence of an unconditional protector is a constant comfort. And although we cannot see this being with our own eyes, a steadfast belief in him infuses us with tremendous energy. I'm convinced that we are all in his palm.

There is no certainty in a promise to ourselves—which is why we make a promise to the Buddha. By doing so, we empower our belief exponentially.

84

BE POSITIVE.

Your mind has the power to decide
whether or not you are happy.

You're here to live out each precious day.

In Japanese history, the Kamakura period (1185–1333) and the early part of the Muromachi period (1333–1392) were characterized by constant warfare. These medieval eras saw the spirit and practice of Zen gain wide support among the samurai class.

The samurai constantly faced down death. They did not know when war would break out—it was quite possible they might fall in battle the very next day.

The spirit of Zen seems perfectly suited to such circumstances. The uncertainty of tomorrow makes it all the more important to live in the moment. One must try one's best to enjoy the present.

In Buddhism we say, "All days are good days," meaning that whether good things happen or bad, each day is precious because it will never come about again. The goodness of every day is determined not by what happens or by whom you meet, but by your own mind.

Any event can be interpreted in multiple ways; what matters is how you respond to it. You may not have any control over what happens or any power to change things, but your reaction is entirely under your control.

Let us make today and every precious day a good day.

85

DO NOT COVET.

*Wanting more
leads to suffering.*

"Is that something I truly need?"

In Buddhism we say *Chisoku*, which means "Be satisfied." Knowing how much is enough is about finding satisfaction in what you already have.

Human desire is endless. Once we acquire one thing, we desire ten of them. And when we acquire ten things, we want a hundred. Even though we know we don't need it, we are unable to rein in our desire. Once engulfed by these feelings, there is no way to satisfy ourselves.

There will be times when we want something we do need. There is nothing wrong with this. But once we acquire the minimum necessary amount, we must learn to tell ourselves, "Ah, this is enough for me."

And then we must keep in check our desire for other things.

Through the practice of *chisoku*, we can achieve a calm and tranquil mind. By simply recognizing that we are fulfilled, our suffering is greatly diminished.

If you find yourself swept up in feelings of dissatisfaction, take a step back and examine what you hope for and desire. And then ask yourself, "Is that something I truly need?"

86

DO NOT DIVIDE THINGS INTO GOOD AND BAD.

Your worries will vanish.

Your breathing is not subject
to judgment—it just is.

There is no particular secret to mastering something. Just repeat the same practice every day. Adopt a sober, steady, continuous routine.

At some point in this routine, you will suddenly realize, "Ah, this is the answer I have been looking for."

A renowned Zen priest will practice his austerities in order to attain enlightenment. An Olympic athlete will persevere with her training by swimming or running.

And then at some point, they will have fulfilled their quest or mastered their art. That's how it works.

By fixating solely on the end point, you will forgo the pleasures of the journey. When you are caught up in producing results, you are unable to devote yourself to the here and now.

By the same token, do not place a value judgment on what you are doing in the moment. Take, for example, breathing: You cannot deem your breathing to be good or bad. Just as you draw one breath after another, perform the routine habitually.

Attempting to define things as good or bad breeds worry and stress.

87

ACCEPT REALITY
FOR WHAT IT IS.

The art of being prepared

It is not about giving up, but about preparing yourself.

The *zenji*, or high priest, Koshu Itabashi is the retired abbot of Sojiji, a temple in Yokohama. He is someone for whom I have tremendous respect.

Itabashi Zenji was informed that he had cancer. Apparently the cancer was quite advanced. And yet every day he continues to dedicate himself to zazen and to asking for alms, as if nothing has changed. "I am now living happily with my cancer," he says.

This is certainly not what one expects to hear.

We cannot change the fact that cancer exists. Though we might struggle and rail against cancer, it remains with us. This is the reality.

So how do we face it? We cannot change what happens in life, but it is within our power to decide how to deal with what happens.

It's about preparing yourself. That is, it's about accepting reality for what it is.

Seeing things as they are. Accepting things as they are.

This might sound like giving up, but in fact it is quite the opposite.

88

THERE IS NOT
JUST ONE ANSWER.

*The meaning behind
Zen koans*

Why do we practice Zen question-and-answering?

These ideas represent the basis of the Buddha's enlightenment:

Our essential self is pure and clean, perfect in its clarity. The search for that essential self is the search for enlightenment, or satori.

As human beings, we possess within us everything we need from the beginning. Enlightenment is not about seeking the answers outside of ourselves, but rather about looking inside. When we encounter our pure and true self, that is enlightenment—satori.

The Rinzai school of Zen Buddhism maintains a rigorous practice of *mondo*—Zen question-and-answering, or the study of Zen koans—in order to attain enlightenment. Koans use language to provoke and test the mind.

Here is a well-known example: "Does a dog have Buddha nature?"

Answering "yes" can be considered wrong, but answering "no" can also be considered wrong.

The practice continues, as more questions that have no answer are posed. With the repetition of this exercise, we come to have insight.

89

THERE IS NOT
JUST ONE WAY, EITHER.

Think with your head?
Or with your body?

We may still arrive at
the same answer.

Whereas the Rinzai school of Zen Buddhism practices koan study to attain enlightenment, the Soto Zen school focuses on zazen and nothing else.

Shikantaza is the Japanese translation of a Chinese colloquialism for zazen, which in English means "single-minded sitting." In *shikantaza*, you forget even that you are sitting, and your mind enters a state of nothingness. You are not seeking enlightenment, you are not strengthening your will, you are not doing this for good health—you aren't actively thinking of anything. In Soto Zen, you simply sit, without striving.

But single-mindedly sitting zazen does have an effect: It hones your wisdom and, after a while, it can lead to enlightenment. The purpose of sitting, though, is not to reach enlightenment—it just so happens that enlightenment is a result of sitting.

Fundamentally, both schools of Zen—Rinzai and Soto— have the same objective: to bring us closer to our essential selves. What differs is simply the methodology by which one achieves it.

Think devotedly with your head? Or think devotedly with your body?

Which style appeals to you?

90

DON'T BE A
SHOW-OFF.

*What charismatic people
have in common*

True charisma comes across
without saying a word.

Some people are so charismatic that others seem naturally attracted to them. It's almost as if they have an aura about them.

At a *zazenkai*, we once discussed the notion of "inhabiting a scent rather than a shape."

The plum tree defies the cold winter, its blossoms giving off an indescribably lovely fragrance. The perfume does not push against the wind—it simply allows itself to be carried along on the current of the breeze. But the scent of a person of virtue wafts in every direction.

A person's charisma or aura is similar.

When people become wealthy, when they rise in status, they tend to become proud and boastful. But their true charisma might come across more naturally if they didn't say a word.

Like the plum blossoms, I try to give off a pleasant scent but not be showy about it. Living graciously "thanks to this person" or knowing that "without that person's help" I wouldn't be where I am today.

91

FREE YOURSELF FROM MONEY.

The more you try to accumulate money,
the more it gets away.

What to focus on in order for
your money worries to subside

Sometimes people ask me, "Buddhist priests don't have to worry about money, do they?" This can be a tricky question to answer.

Even though I'm the chief priest of a temple, money is still a requirement. I have a family, and there are basic necessities I must buy.

According to Zen teaching, soliciting money is not wrong in and of itself, but it mustn't take on too much importance.

The founder of the Soto school of Zen Buddhism, Dogen Zenji, warned us that those committed to an ascetic Buddhist lifestyle must not allow themselves to be tempted by fame or fortune. We must not seek to enrich our reputation or our pockets.

The strange thing about money is this: The more attached we become to it, the more it eludes our grasp. Instead of thinking about money, we should concern ourselves with our higher purpose.

How can I contribute to society? What can I do to be useful in the world? By contemplating these questions and taking action, you'll find that the money you need will ultimately find you.

92

BELIEVE IN YOURSELF, ESPECIALLY WHEN YOU FEEL ANXIOUS.

*Focus on the self-confidence that
lies behind the anxiety.*

There are two sides to anxiety.

Imagine that you've studied your hardest for the school entrance exam, and the day of the exam has finally arrived.

Or that you've put time and effort into preparing a presentation, and now it's showtime.

Although you hope to do your best, at the very last minute you are hit by a wave of anxiety. For some people, it may be that the harder they try, the more anxious they feel.

When that happens, take a look at what lies beneath the anxiety. I expect that what you will find is self-confidence.

Once you can recognize the self-confidence beneath your anxiety, you will be able to overcome whatever anxiety you may be seized by.

This is why it is so important to make a habit of believing in yourself.

It is often said that if you want to develop confidence in yourself, the first and most difficult challenge is to stretch the limits of your own mind. Doing so will lead to a sense of accomplishment, and little by little your accomplishments will boost your confidence.

Everything will be all right.

You've made it this far already, haven't you?

93

NOTICE THE CHANGES
OF THE SEASON.

It will inspire you to go on.

Herein lies the only truth in the world.

However much the world changes, there are some things that remain the same.

Namely, spring will arrive and the buds will sprout, and then autumn will descend and the leaves will fall. In other words, things will take their natural course. This is exactly what is meant by the character for the Buddha in Buddhism—仏—which signifies bliss, or the "Buddha nature" of things.

What we call spring actually has no physical form. Spring does not materially exist.

Nevertheless, when winter comes to an end, the northern wind shifts to a southern breeze, bringing warmer temperatures. Soon the plants sprout buds. We see this and think to ourselves, "Ah, spring has arrived."

But perhaps there are those who don't notice the buds and flowers, or some who see them and feel nothing—for these people, there is no such thing as spring.

A Chinese poet from the Northern Song dynasty named Su Shi was struck by the beauty of the spring landscape and said, "The willows in their green, the flowers in their crimson, reveal their true nature." In the natural shape of things—this is where the truth is found.

With an open mind, notice the truth in the everyday—in the Buddha nature of things.

This awareness will give us the courage we need to go on living.

94

TRY TAKING CARE
OF SOMETHING.

Develop affection for
someone or something.

*Understand what is
important in life.*

Nowadays, more and more people are getting back to nature.

They buy land in the countryside and on their days off they devote themselves to working in the field. Or they start a small garden in their yard, growing vegetables and flowers. I think all of this is wonderful.

You cultivate the land and plant seeds. You worry when the weather remains dry and fret when there's too much rain. This is not merely about the simple act of growing plants— it's about savoring the time and effort that goes into it.

When whatever it is you are growing begins to thrive, you feel unreservedly happy. And also relieved. However much affection you put into it, the object of your affection gives you back energy in equal measure.

You might even think of what you're cultivating as a stand-in for yourself. When that happens, not a drop of the affection you give goes to waste.

When you buy a tomato at the market, it's just another tomato to you. But a tomato that was grown with your own hands transcends being a simple "ingredient."

It is through the act of nurturing something that we develop a mind that cares for things, a mind that feels affection for others.

95

LISTEN FOR THE VOICE
OF YOUR TRUE SELF.

Learn to appreciate this insight.

*A dry landscape garden
symbolizes a life of seclusion.*

One of the buildings of a Zen temple is the abbot's quarters, called a *hojo*. Historically there has always been a Zen garden attached to the *hojo*.

Why do you think the chief priest has his own ideal little garden, right outside of where he lives?

Most Zen gardens are dry landscape gardens—called *kare-sansui*. Long ago, the ideal lifestyle for a Zen monk was to seclude himself deep in the mountains, in order to devote himself to spiritual training. Perhaps there was enjoyment in living as a hermit, like the famous monk Ryokan from the Edo period.

But in truth it is very difficult to live this way. Nowadays few monks seclude themselves deep in the mountains, but they have dry landscape gardens to symbolize this ideal.

Perhaps this will deepen your appreciation of Zen gardens.

The next time you visit one, take a moment to sit and imagine you have wandered deep within the mountains.

Transported in this way, liberated from your daily obligations, your mind becomes transparent and your true self may unexpectedly reveal itself.

96

CHERISH BEING ALIVE, EVERY SINGLE DAY.

*Life really does go by
in the blink of an eye.*

*Time spent out of character
is empty time.*

In Zen temples, there is a wooden board called a *han* that is struck with a mallet to signal that it is time for some part of the daily routine. It might have the words *Shoji jidai* written on it in ink. Have you ever seen this? The words mean "Life is full of fortune and misfortune, but cherish being alive, every single day. Life will pass you by."

My father belonged to the generation that experienced war when they were young.

He once found himself in the middle of an exchange of gunfire. It was a furious attack by the enemy. My father lay flat on the ground, desperately trying to escape the fusillade. When the shots finally stopped and he dared raise his head, his fellow soldiers on either side were dead. Whenever my father told this story, he always ended it by saying, "I am grateful to be alive and to be here today. We human beings are enlivened by a great and invisible power."

We are enlivened—we are given life. And for that reason, we must not waste it.

We must see our true selves with an open mind, and when we think of things—when there are things we want to do—we must do them as if our lives depend on it. Time spent out of character is empty time.

Come now, open your eyes.

What kind of day should we make today?

97

PUT YOUR EVERYTHING
INTO THE HERE AND NOW.

Life is a long but brief practice.

My father,
who lived every day to the utmost

My father lived to the ripe old age of eighty-seven. For several years before his death, he suffered from cancer, but to have lived that long, it's almost as if he had died of "natural cancer."

The day before he passed away, my father spent three hours weeding the temple garden. The day he passed away, he rose early as always, tidied his room, and did the sweeping.

After lunch, he felt a bit dizzy and bumped his chest against the table, so he went to the hospital to get checked out. They took his blood pressure, which turned out to be abnormally low, and it was shortly after they administered an IV drip to raise his blood pressure that he passed away quietly.

To me, that is such a beautiful way to die. I don't imagine I'll ever live up to my father.

He was simply single-minded about living in the moment. Up until the day he passed away, he devoted himself to tending the garden, and to the utmost of his ability he tried to carry out the responsibilities he was entrusted with.

Perhaps my father had a premonition of his death. But it would have been something that only he had known.

He taught me, through his example, that the practice continues up until the moment of your death.

98

MAKE EVERY PREPARATION.

Destiny comes for all of us.

There are those who seize opportunities,
and those who let them pass.

Here is a Zen parable:

There are two plum trees. One had been preparing itself throughout the cold winter, so that when the spring breeze arrived it would be ready and able to bloom. The other one started to think about blooming only once the spring breeze arrived; this tree was still shivering in the cold when suddenly the warmer wind began to blow. The plum tree that was prepared grabbed the chance for its flowers to burst open, whereas the other one took that as the moment to begin preparations for its blossoms.

The very next day, the spring breeze was gone, and winter's cold returned. In the end, the blossoms on the plum tree that neglected its preparations were unable to fully bloom that year.

It's just the same with people.

The winds of destiny blow for all of us. Whether you are able to make the most of an opportunity will depend upon long-standing dedication and preparedness.

99

CONTEMPLATE HOW TO DIE.

Whenever you are confused
about how to live

Happiness is right at hand.

The word *shoji* is Japanese for the Buddhist concept of samsara, the cycle of death and rebirth.

We are born into this world, and then we die. These are simply two sides of the same experience. In other words, just as we contemplate how to live, we should contemplate how to die.

If you were told that your life were going to end in six months, you would probably give a considerable amount of thought to how you wanted to spend that time. But what if it were only a month? A week? What if your life were to end tomorrow? Surely, right then, you would know what you should do in that moment. You would feel as though you mustn't waste today.

Life happens in the blink of an eye. It really is just like that.

Have you ever spent a day off watching television and, before you even noticed, discovered that it was evening? "Ah," you may have thought to yourself, "I didn't mean to waste so much time." When you want to get something done, or you want to put your mind to something, time spent not focused on anything in particular feels like wasted time.

We must do our best not to squander this "blink of an eye" that has been given to us.

100

MAKE THE MOST OF LIFE.

Life is a precious thing,
for our safekeeping.

Your life is your own,
but it is not your possession.

This may seem out of the blue, but whose life is it anyway?

To those who immediately reply, "My life is definitely mine," let's think about that for a moment.

In Buddhism, the word *jomyo* means one's predestined life span. Each of us has our own *jomyo*. From the moment we are born, the length of our lifetime is determined. But none of us knows how long it will be.

In other words, being alive means we must make the most of the life we are entrusted with. Life is not ours to possess— it is a precious gift that we must treat as if it were placed in our care. And whatever life span we are given, we must take the utmost care to give it back.

Some among us will be graced with a long life, and others may have only a brief amount of time. There is nothing fair about this.

But Buddhism teaches that a life's worth is not measured by its duration.

What is important is how we use the life we are given.

How will you use your life today?